It's another quality book from CGP...

Help is at hand for Grade 9-1 GCSE Religious Studies — this fantastic CGP book is perfectly tailored to Christianity, Catholic Christianity and Islam!

It's packed with crystal-clear study notes for the AQA A exam, plus plenty of exam-style questions to make sure you're ready for the real thing.

How to access your free Online Edition

This book includes a free Online Edition to read on your PC, Mac or tablet. To access it, just go to **cgpbooks.co.uk/extras** and enter this code...

0657 3659 3838 6715

By the way, this code only works for one person. If somebody else has used this book before you, they might have already claimed the Online Edition.

CGP — still the best! ☺

Our sole aim here at CGP is to produce the highest quality books — carefully written, immaculately presented and dangerously close to being funny.

Then we work our socks off to get them out to you — at the cheapest possible prices.

Contents

Theme C — The Existence of God and Revelation

Theme D — Religion, Peace and Conflict

Theme E — Religion, Crime and Punishment

Theme F — Religion, Human Rights and Social Justice

Theme G — St Mark's Gospel: the Life of Jesus

Theme H — St Mark's Gospel as a Source of Religious, Moral and Spiritual Truths

---

The green religion tags on the pages of each section tell you whether the page covers:

| Christianity | ...information about a specific religion... | Christianity & Islam | ...information about both religions... | General | ...or general information. |

Published by CGP

Editors: Ellen Burton, Robbie Driscoll, Daniel Fielding, Sam Norman, Caroline Purvis

Contributors: Paul Smith, Philip West

Proofreading: Glenn Rogers

ISBN: 978 1 78908 570 9

With thanks to Emily Smith for the copyright research.

Sacred Text References

References from the Bible always go in the order: Book Chapter:Verse(s). So whenever you see something like: Genesis 1:14, it means it's from the book of Genesis, Chapter 1, verse 14.

Similarly, references from the Qur'an are shown with the Surah (Chapter) followed by the Ayah (Verse).

For all collections of hadith, we've used the English referencing system. This gives the book number followed by the hadith number, e.g. Sahih al-Bukhari 1:3.

Scripture quotations [marked NIV] taken from the Holy Bible,
New International Version Anglicised
Copyright © 1979, 1984, 2011 Biblica, Used by permission of Hodder & Stoughton Ltd, an Hachette UK company
All rights reserved
'NIV' is a registered trademark of Biblica
UK trademark number 1448790.

Holy Qur'an quotations taken from the Holy Qur'an, Sahih International Version. https://quran.com/

Quotations from the Catechism of the Catholic Church © Libreria Editrice Vaticana

Quotations from Lumen gentium on page 16, Gaudium et spes on page 20, Evangelii Gaudium on pages 21 and 22, Humanae Vitae on pages 38 and 52, Familiaris Consortio on pages 42, 43 and 45, and a speech by Pope Francis on page 47 © Libreria Editrice Vaticana

With thanks to Alamy for permission to use the images on page 13: Photo of Quaker meeting house © John Morrison / Alamy Stock Photo, photo of evangelical church worship © Julio Etchart / Alamy Stock Photo and the image on page 52 © Isabelle Plasschaert / Alamy Stock Photo.

Source of statistic on belief in evolution on page 56: Theos

Sahih Muslim 16:4152 quote on page 78 from https://muflihun.com

Quote by Muhammad on page 82 from Islam and the West: A Rational Perspective by Mohammed Jabar, published by Mereo Books, an imprint of Memoirs Publishing, 2014.

Data about wealth inequality on page 86 contains public sector information licensed under the Open Government Licence v3.0. http://www.nationalarchives.gov.uk/doc/open-government-licence/version/3/

Every effort has been made to locate copyright holders and obtain permission to reproduce sources. For those sources where it has been difficult to trace the originator of the work, we would be grateful for information. If any copyright holder would like us to make an amendment to the acknowledgements, please notify us and we will gladly update the book at the next reprint. Thank you.

Printed by Elanders Ltd, Newcastle upon Tyne
Clipart from Corel®

Based on the classic CGP style created by Richard Parsons.

Introduction to Christianity

Christianity is based on the belief in **Jesus Christ** being the **Son of God**. It is the **main** religion in Britain.

The Bible is the Christian sacred text

The Bible is divided into two main parts — the **Old** and **New Testaments**:

OLD TESTAMENT	

- Depending on the version, the **Old Testament** has at least 39 books, which include the **Creation** story (see p.4-5) and the **Ten Commandments**.
- These 39 books are the **Jewish scriptures** — they are also considered **sacred** by Jews.

NEW TESTAMENT

- The New Testament is the part of the Bible that is specifically Christian.
- Its 27 books include the **4 Gospels** (Matthew, Mark, Luke and John), which are accounts of Jesus's life.
- The Acts of the Apostles and the letters of St Paul describe the early years of Christianity.

Christianity is divided into different traditions

The different branches of Christianity are called **denominations**. They share key beliefs, but interpret some points of the faith differently and worship in different ways (see pages 12-13).

Roman Catholics
- **Roman Catholics** respect the authority of the **Bible** and **Church tradition**, plus the authority of the **Pope** and his teachings.
- The **seven sacraments** (which include the Eucharist — see p.14) are an important part of their faith.

Orthodox Christians
- **Orthodox Christians** are found mainly in Eastern Europe, Russia and Greece.
- They also have **7 sacraments**, and honour (but don't worship) **icons** — pictures of Saints.

Protestants
- **Protestants** base their beliefs and practices on the **Bible**, rather than Church tradition or the teachings of the Pope.
- In England and Wales, Protestant denominations that are not part of the 'Anglican Communion' are often called 'Nonconformists'.

    These include Methodists, Baptists, Pentecostals, The Society of Friends (Quakers) and the Salvation Army.

The **Church of England** has both Roman Catholic and Protestant features. Its beliefs are set out in the **39 Articles**. Anglicanism is the worldwide 'communion' of Churches in fellowship with the parent Church of England.

The New Testament — not so new these days...

It's important to remember what a diverse range of traditions there is within Christianity. You need to know about contrasting religious beliefs for the exam, but that doesn't always mean writing about different religions — you can also compare Christian denominations too.

Christianity & Catholic Christianity

Introduction to Christianity

There are many beliefs about the nature of God

- Christianity is a **monotheistic** (one God) religion. The Ten Commandments say:

> **"You shall have no other gods"** *(Exodus 20:3 NIV)*

- Christians believe God has the following **characteristics**:

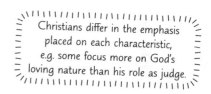
Christians differ in the emphasis placed on each characteristic, e.g. some focus more on God's loving nature than his role as judge.

OMNIPOTENT 	God is **all-powerful**, although he still allows each person **free will**.

BENEVOLENT	God is **loving** and **caring**: > **"For God so loved the world that he gave his one and only Son."** *John 3:16 NIV* Christians try to **follow** his example in their actions.

JUST JUDGE 	• God **judges** people's actions fairly. • Those who reject him and live sinful lives will be **punished**, as shown in the story of the sheep and goats in Matthew 25:31-46 (see p.22). • But God **forgives** people who are sorry for what they've done and become faithful to him — the story of the **prodigal son** (Luke 15:11-32) shows God will forgive anyone who returns to his ways.

ETERNAL 	God has always existed, and he will continue to exist **forever**.	**TRANSCENDENT** 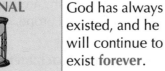	God is **beyond** this world — he doesn't depend on it to exist.

OMNISCIENT ∞	God **knows** everything — in the past, present and future.	**IMMANENT** 	God is **present** in the human world, and takes an **active role** in humanity.

PERSONAL	• God is a '**person**', albeit an almighty and **divine person**. • If God is personal, then a relationship is possible through **prayer** — which can be a '**conversation**' with God.

Omnipotent or omniscient? Get them the right way round...

That might seem like an awful lot of characteristics, but it's important to know them all if you want to get a good idea of how Christians perceive God. So have a go at covering this page and seeing how many of them you can write down from memory. No peeking...

Beliefs, Teachings and Practices — Christianity & Catholic Christianity

The Trinity

Although Christians believe in one God, they also believe that God has three parts.

Christians believe in God as the Trinity

The Trinity is the idea that God exists in three 'persons' — the Father, the Son (Jesus) and the Holy Spirit.
The importance of all three is shown in the Bible:

> "[Jesus] saw the Spirit of God descending like a dove and alighting on him. And a voice from heaven said, 'This is my Son, whom I love; with him I am well pleased.' " *Matthew 3:16-17 NIV*

This happened at Jesus's baptism.

> "[Jesus has] equality with God" *Philippians 2:6 NIV*

St Paul described Jesus this way.

The Trinity is explained in the Nicene Creed

In 325 AD, Church leaders from around the world gathered at the **Council of Nicaea**.
They produced a **creed** — a statement of beliefs. This was further developed at the **Council of Constinople** in 381 AD, and is known as the **Nicene Creed**. It describes how Christians see God:

> "We believe in one God, the Father, the Almighty, maker of heaven and earth... We believe in one Lord, Jesus Christ, the only Son of God... of one Being with the Father... was made man... he suffered death and... he rose again... We believe in the Holy Spirit... the giver of life, who proceeds from the Father and the Son... who has spoken through the prophets." *Nicene Creed*

- Before this, not everyone had **agreed** that the Son of God (Jesus) was **one with God**, rather than having been **made by God**. Now they agreed that he was **equally** important.
- The **importance** the **early Church** placed on the **Trinity** in the Nicene Creed means it is a **key belief** for most Christians — but some groups, such as **Christadelphians**, don't believe in the Trinity.
- Christians see the three parts of the Trinity as having **different characteristics** and **roles**:

For many Christians, **God the Father** is the God of the **Old Testament**. He **created** Heaven and Earth and **sustains** them. **God the Father** might be described as the **transcendent part** of God.

The title 'Father' is a mark of **respect** for God, and is used by Jesus in the Gospels:

> "Be perfect, therefore, as your heavenly Father is perfect." *Matthew 5:48 NIV*

Christians believe that the **Holy Spirit** is the **presence** of God in the world. Before his death, Jesus promised his disciples:

> "I will ask the Father, and he will give you another advocate to help you and be with you for ever — the Spirit of truth." *John 14:16-17 NIV*

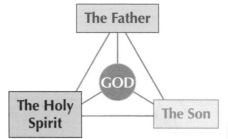

Christians believe Jesus (see p.9-11) is the incarnation of God in human form. He is seen as both divine and human — the immanent and personal part of God, who understands human suffering.

Christians believe that Jesus provides a model for Christian behaviour in obedience to God the Father.

The Holy Spirit is seen as the **immanent yet impersonal** part of God — it continues to **guide** the **Church**.

Some Christians feel that the Holy Spirit also guides them **personally** in being good Christians.

> "By this power of the Spirit, God's children can bear much fruit." *Catechism of the Catholic Church 736*

The Gospels contain a record of his life and teachings, and are an important source of guidance for Christians on how they should live their lives.

Three into one doesn't go in maths — but this is RS...

For the 5 mark exam questions, you're going to have to refer to sacred texts. You can write quotes, or just paraphrase what is said. Say where it comes from, e.g. which book of the Bible.

Creation

The story of creation can be understood in different ways. Some take it **literally**, for others it's a **metaphor**.

The Bible describes how God created the universe

Genesis chapter 1 says that **God** created everything.
The process took **six days**, and on the seventh day God **rested**:

Day 1
Light and **darkness** were made.

Day 2
The **sky** was made.

Day 3
Oceans, **land** and **plants** on the land were created.
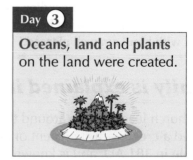

Day 4
The **sun**, **moon** and **stars** were created.

Day 5
The creatures of the water and sky (e.g. **fish** and **birds**) were created.
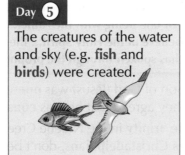

Day 6
Land animals and **people** were created.

Day 7
God rested.
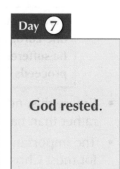

All the beings of the Holy Trinity were involved

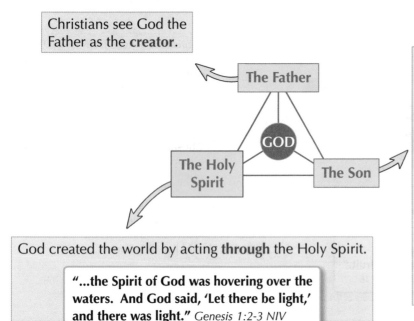

Christians see God the Father as the **creator**.

The role of the **Son of God** is described in the Gospel of John. He uses the phrase '**the Word**', but it is clear he is referring to **Jesus** as he later says, *"The Word became flesh and made his dwelling among us"* (John 1:14 NIV). John makes it clear that Jesus was **vital for creation**.

> "In the beginning was the Word, and the Word was with God, and the Word was God. He was with God in the beginning. Through him all things were made; without him nothing was made that has been made." *John 1:1-3 NIV*

God created the world by acting **through** the Holy Spirit.

> "...the Spirit of God was hovering over the waters. And God said, 'Let there be light,' and there was light." *Genesis 1:2-3 NIV*

Creation

The Bible explains how human beings were created

The creation of human beings is described in Genesis chapters 1 and 2.
The first two humans were Adam and Eve, and they lived in the Garden of Eden.

> "So God created mankind in his own image, in the image of God he created them; male and female he created them." *Genesis 1:27 NIV*

> "The Lord God formed a man from the dust of the ground." *Genesis 2:7 NIV*

> "[God] made a woman from the rib he had taken out of man." *Genesis 2:7 NIV*

The fact that God created humans in his image is important:
- Because of this, Christians believe that humans are special. They think humans should behave like God by being loving and fair (see p.1).
- It also shows that humans are important to God, and so everyone should be treated with respect.

> "Rule over the fish in the sea and the birds in the sky and over every living creature that moves on the ground." *Genesis 1:28 NIV*

God gave this instruction to Adam and Eve. Some Christians believe this means God gave humans 'dominion' (power) over his creation and they can use it as they like.

> "The Lord God took the man and put him in the Garden of Eden to work it and take care of it." *Genesis 2:15 NIV*

Many Christians interpret this as humans having 'stewardship' of the Earth — God expects them to care for it.

There are different ways to interpret the creation story

Some Christians take the creation story literally...
- They are known as creationists.
- They believe that the process took six days, and humans are descended from Adam and Eve.

Other Christians are more liberal in their understanding of the Bible's events...
- They view Genesis as more of a parable, or a symbolic description.
- They acknowledge God as the creator, but are open to other theories, such as the Big Bang theory and evolution. These theories can offer more information to Christians about how God made the universe. The Roman Catholic Church has accepted both theories.

The creation story can help Christians further understand God's nature:

Eternal ⟹ God is eternal as he made time, and was present 'prior' to it.

Omnipotent ⟹ He is omnipotent as he created the universe through words.

Benevolent ⟹ God's benevolence can be seen through creation too as he brought humankind to life and gave them the world.

And you thought revision was tiring...

Grab a pen and paper and see if you can summarise what Genesis chapters 1 and 2 say about the creation. Once you've done that, try jotting down some different interpretations of creation.

Evil and Suffering

Evil comes in **different forms**, and can have an **impact** on a person's relationship with their faith.

Free will led to evil entering the world

- **Christianity** teaches that evil **entered** the world as a result of **Adam and Eve** giving in to **temptation** in the Garden of Eden — they **disobeyed** God by eating the **fruit** of the tree of knowledge.

> "When the woman saw... the fruit of the tree... she took some and ate it. She also gave some to her husband... and he ate it." *Genesis 3:6 NIV*

'The Fall'	original sin
the switch from a perfect world to one containing evil after Adam and Eve disobeyed God	*the idea that, after the Fall, every human being was born with a flawed nature, capable of causing suffering*

- Christians believe God created humans with **free will**.
- It's up to humans to **choose** whether they perform evil deeds or not.
- This is shown in the story of **Adam and Eve** and how it was up to them whether to give in to temptation or not.
- **Good** is the opposite of **evil**, and since God is good, Christians try to follow his **example**.

Evil can be either human-made or natural

Evil and suffering can be divided into **two types**:

1 Moral (human-made) Evil

- This is when suffering is brought about by the **cruel** actions of **people**.
- This includes things like murder, war, rape and torture.
- The person causing the evil is able to make a **choice** about what is morally **right or wrong**.

2 Natural Evil

- This kind of evil, and the suffering that comes with it, is **caused by the world** in which we live, and is **no one's 'fault'**.
- This includes lots of things, but some examples include disease, floods, earthquakes and hurricanes.
- However, many **recent natural disasters** may have been caused by **human interference** in the natural world, raising the question of whether that makes those events human-made.

Evil and Suffering

Evil can lead people to question their faith

- **Evil** and **suffering** may lead some people to **question** their belief in God — or even to **reject** their faith:

> Since suffering exists, God **can't** be **both** benevolent and omnipotent — a loving and all-powerful God wouldn't **allow** it to happen. This means that God **doesn't exist**, or he can't have the **characteristics** that believers say he has.

> "the Lord is compassionate and gracious, slow to anger, abounding in love... he does not treat us as our sins deserve..."
> *Psalm 103:8-10 NIV*

- Christians **react** to the problem of evil and suffering in various ways:

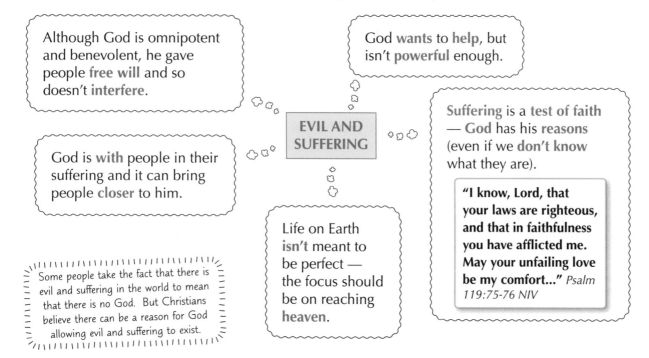

> Although God is omnipotent and benevolent, he gave people **free will** and so doesn't **interfere**.

> God **wants** to **help**, but isn't **powerful** enough.

> **EVIL AND SUFFERING**

> God is **with** people in their suffering and it can bring people **closer** to him.

> **Suffering** is a **test of faith** — **God** has his **reasons** (even if we **don't know** what they are).

> "I know, Lord, that your laws are righteous, and that in faithfulness you have afflicted me. May your unfailing love be my comfort..." *Psalm 119:75-76 NIV*

> Life on Earth **isn't** meant to be perfect — the focus should be on reaching **heaven**.

> Some people take the fact that there is evil and suffering in the world to mean that there is no God. But Christians believe there can be a reason for God allowing evil and suffering to exist.

The Book of Job teaches that suffering must be accepted

- The **Book of Job** tells of the **terrible suffering** Job endures and how he **questions** God. In the end, Job comes to the conclusion that God is **all-powerful** and knows what he is doing — and that suffering must be **accepted** because people can't really **understand** the world or **God's plan**.

> "Though he slay me, yet will I hope in him..."
> *Job 13:15 NIV*

- Christians believe they should try to **help** people who are suffering — **practically** (charity) and by **praying**. Jesus said that *"...whatever you did for one of... these brothers and sisters of mine, you did for me"* (Matthew 25:40 NIV).

 Not the cheeriest of topics...
Christians explain and respond to evil and suffering in a variety of ways.
Cover this page, see how many you can think of and write them all down.

The Afterlife

What people believe will happen to them after **death** can influence the way they **live** their lives.

Christians believe in heaven and hell

- Christianity teaches that the **soul** lives on after death (**immortality** of the soul), and that the body will be **resurrected** (brought back to life) for Judgement Day, just as Jesus was resurrected after his crucifixion.

- Christians believe God will judge you and you'll go to **heaven** or **hell**:

> **life after death**
> *the idea that, although your body may die, your soul can live on after death*

Heaven is often portrayed as a place of great beauty and serenity, a **paradise** where you'll spend eternity with God — as long as you believe in Jesus and have followed his **teachings**, you can be saved by **God's grace** (see p.11). The **soul** can go to heaven even though the body ('earthly tent') is gone.

> **"I am the resurrection and the life. The one who believes in me will live, even though they die..."** *John 11:25 NIV*

> **"For we know that if the earthly tent we live in is destroyed, we have a building from God, an eternal house in heaven, not built by human hands."** *2 Corinthians 5:1 NIV*

Hell, on the other hand, is often portrayed as a place of **torment** and **pain** — the final destination of **nonbelievers** and those who have led **bad** lives.

> **"Then they will go away to eternal punishment, but the righteous to eternal life."** *Matthew 25:46 NIV*

- However, not all Christians believe that heaven and hell are **real** places — many see heaven and hell as **states of mind**. In heaven you'll be **happy**, and know God — in hell you'll be **unable** to know God's love. Pope John Paul II said that hell was a **metaphor** for how people who've **rejected** God will **feel**.

Some Christians, for example Roman Catholics, believe that going to hell means that any **connection** they have to God will be **severed** forever.

> **"This state of definitive self-exclusion from communion with God... is called 'hell'"** *Catechism of the Catholic Church 1033*

| Purgatory |

Read this if you're studying Catholic Christianity.

Roman Catholics believe in a place, or state of existence, called **Purgatory**. Here **sins** are punished and the person must *"undergo purification"* (Catechism of the Catholic Church, 1030) before the soul can move on to heaven. Protestants believe this isn't in the Bible, so they **reject** it.

Some believe God **wouldn't** punish people for **eternity**.

A few believe that those who God finds **unacceptable** will be **annihilated**. In a report called 'The Mystery of Salvation', senior members of the **Church of England** said that for those people *"the only end is **total non-being**"*.

Some believe that a loving God **wouldn't** allow anyone to go to hell.

Christians believe resurrection happens at the Last Judgement

- Many Christians believe that Jesus will return to Earth in the **Second Coming** (**Parousia**), and everyone who has died will be **resurrected**.

> **"Christ... ascended into Heaven, and there sitteth, until he return to judge all Men at the last day."** *39 Articles IV*

- Some believe that all of humanity will then be judged at the **Last Judgement**. Those that God finds **acceptable** will enter **heaven** — the rest will go to hell, as in the story of the sheep and the goats (Matthew 25:31-46).

> **"in Christ all will be made alive"** *1 Corinthians 15:22 NIV*

> **"For we must all appear before the judgement seat of Christ, so that each of us may receive what is due to us for the things done while in the body, whether good or bad."** *2 Corinthians 5:10 NIV*

Some Christians, e.g. Roman Catholics, believe in a **personal** day of **judgement** straight after a person **dies** — their actions will be judged and they'll go to heaven or hell **straight away**.

Some think they'll be **judged again** at the Last Judgement, and will **re-enter** heaven or hell in their **resurrected forms**.

Others don't believe in a personal judgement — the soul must **wait** to be judged at the **Last Judgement**.

The examiners will be judging your answers...

Explain two Christian beliefs about judgement. Give examples to illustrate your answer. [5]

Jesus Christ and Salvation

Christians believe that Jesus Christ, the second Person of the Trinity, is the **Son of God**.

God became *human* at the *incarnation*

- The **incarnation** was the act by which **God** became a **human being** as Jesus Christ.
- An **angel** told a woman called **Mary** in Nazareth that she would have a **son** — and that *"the holy one to be born will be called the Son of God"* (Luke 1:35 NIV).

> **"he... was incarnate from the Holy Spirit and the Virgin Mary and was made man"** *Nicene Creed*

JESUS

- Christians don't believe that Jesus was 'half God and half man' — he was **fully both**. The Bible describes how God *"appeared in the flesh"* (1 Timothy 3:16 NIV).

> **"The Word became flesh and made his dwelling among us. We have seen his glory, the glory of the one and only Son, who came from the Father, full of grace and truth."** *John 1:14 NIV*

- Jesus is referred to as '**Christ**' or '**Messiah**' — the '**Anointed One of God**'.
- Christians see Jesus's time on Earth as God's way of showing how much he **loves** the world. They study the **Gospels** to find out about **Jesus's life**, and to see how they should live their own.

After being baptised by John the Baptist, Jesus began **teaching**. He had many followers, including **12 chosen disciples**.

Some of his key teachings are in the **Sermon on the Mount** (Matthew 5-7) — he taught how the poor and meek are **highly valued** by God, and how **peacemakers** are blessed.

He also taught the importance of **kindness**, such as in the story of the **Good Samaritan** (Luke 10:30-37).

He performed miracles such as **healing** the sick and bringing people **back to life**, showing that he was the **Son of God** and demonstrating God's **love**.

Jesus Christ and Salvation

Salvation is needed before Christians can go to heaven, and **Jesus's actions** made it possible.

Jesus was crucified and resurrected

The Last Supper, Jesus's Arrest and Trial

- Shortly before his death, Jesus and his disciples ate their **Passover** meal in Jerusalem. It was their **final meal** together and became known as the **Last Supper**.

- At the meal, Jesus gave the disciples **bread** saying *"this is my body"* and **wine** saying *"This is my blood"* (Mark 14:22-24 NIV). Luke's Gospel tells us he said *"do this in remembrance of me"* (Luke 22:19 NIV). These words are important to many Christians today who remember Jesus with bread and wine through the **Eucharist** (p.14).

- At the Last Supper, Jesus also **washed** his disciples' **feet**, which teaches Christians about how important it is to **serve** others.

- After the Last Supper, Jesus went to pray in the **Garden of Gethsemane**, where he was **arrested**. The authorities felt **threatened** by Jesus — earlier that week, crowds had called him the '**King of Israel**'.

- He was put on **trial** before the Jewish **high priest** and found guilty of **blasphemy**. Then Jesus was tried before the Roman governor, **Pilate** — he offered to release Jesus, but the crowd said *"Crucify him!"* (Mark 15:13 NIV). He was **flogged**, before being sent to die.

Crucifixion

- Jesus was **crucified** at a place called **Golgotha**, next to two robbers. A sign was fixed to Jesus's cross that read 'The King of the Jews', to record the **charge** against him. Passers-by threw **insults** at Jesus, saying that he could **save others**, but couldn't **save himself**.

- In his suffering, Jesus cried out, *"My God, my God, why have you forsaken me?"* (Mark 15:34 NIV). This shows that Jesus understands how people can feel abandoned in their **suffering**.

- Christians also believe the crucifixion helped to **repair** the **relationship** between God and mankind — the **atonement** (see next page).

Resurrection

- After the crucifixion, Jesus's body was put in a tomb. But he was **resurrected** (brought back to life), and his tomb was found **empty**.

- Jesus talked to two women and told them *"Go and tell my brothers to go to Galilee; there they will see me"* (Matthew 28:10 NIV).

- The resurrection is important to Christians as it shows them that there is **life after death** — **death** becomes **less frightening**.

- It shows them just how **powerful** God is. This power that raised Jesus from the dead gives people the **strength** to live Christian lives.

- Christians also see the resurrection as further **proof** that Jesus is the **Son of God** as he was *"...appointed the Son of God in power by his resurrection from the dead..."* (Romans 1:4 NIV). This strengthens people's **faith**.

> *"...Why do you look for the living among the dead? He is not here; he has risen!"*
> *Luke 24:5-6 NIV*

Roman Catholics refer to the crucifixion, resurrection and ascension of Jesus as 'The Paschal Mystery'.

Jesus going to heaven is called the ascension

- Over the **40 days** after the resurrection, many of Jesus's disciples said they had met him **alive** in various places around **Jerusalem**.

- Then, Jesus '**ascended into Heaven**' to be with God the Father once again. He had **done** what he was sent to **Earth** to do, and it was time for him to **go back** to God.

- In John 14:2, Jesus tells his disciples he will *"prepare a place"* (NIV) for them in heaven. 1 John 2:1 says that, in Jesus, Christians have an 'advocate' with God (someone who will look out for them).

- **Pope Benedict XVI** said that since **Jesus** was **human** and went to be with God, the **ascension** shows there's a **place** for all human beings **with God**.

- The ascension shows **Jesus's power** — he is now *"at the right hand of the mighty God"* (Luke 22:69 NIV).

> *"While he was blessing them, he left them and was taken up into heaven."*
> *Luke 24:51 NIV*

Jesus Christ and Salvation

Jesus died to save humanity

- **'Original sin'** (see p.6) means that **everyone** is born capable of sin. Many Christians believe that Jesus's **suffering** and **death** won **forgiveness** for everyone and ensured their **redemption** (freeing them from sin).
- They believe that Jesus was **perfect** (without sin), but God placed **all the sins of the world** on him at his crucifixion. Romans 3:21-26 teaches that his sacrifice **paid** for their sins, so long as they have **faith** in him.
- Jesus's actions brought about the **reconciliation** between God and humanity — known as the **atonement**.
- His power and goodness were so **great** that after he was crucified, death couldn't keep hold of him.
- However, **not** all Christians believe that Jesus **had to die** to pay for people's sins:

> "For God so loved the world that he gave his one and only Son, that whoever believes in him shall not perish but have eternal life. For God did not send his Son into the world to condemn the world, but to save the world through him."
> *John 3:16-17 NIV*

> 1 Corinthians 13:5 says that love *"keeps no record of wrongs"* (NIV). Many Christians think that Jesus's death **wasn't required** for a loving and merciful God to be able to **forgive** people's sins.

> Some people argue that it was Jesus's **ministry** that showed people how to be free from sin — he showed them how to live their lives in a **Godly** way.

> Some say Jesus's death shows **God's love** for humankind through his **willingness** to **suffer** and die as humans do. His resurrection showed how God could **triumph** over **sin** and **death**, so people don't have to fear **evil**.

Christians must seek salvation to get to heaven

- To achieve salvation, Christians believe they must have faith in Jesus.

> "Salvation is found in no one else..." *Acts 4:12 NIV*

- Salvation is only possible through God's grace — God showing favour to those who **haven't** earned it.

> "For it is by grace you have been saved, through faith... it is the gift of God" *Ephesians 2:8 NIV*

salvation
the soul being saved from death and sin, allowing it to reach heaven

BUT...

People can't just **say** they believe — if they're a true believer they'll try to **live** a Christian life. The Bible contains many **laws**, such as the **Ten Commandments**, which provide Christians with **guidance** on how they should behave. Everyone will **sin**, but the laws mean they'll *"become conscious of ... sin"* (Romans 3:20 NIV) and *"turn to God in repentance"* (Acts 20:21 NIV).

- The Holy Spirit helps Christians to follow the teachings of God and his laws and keep their faith, helping them to find salvation.

Revision can save you from exam failure...

'Jesus's death had to happen in order to save humanity.' Evaluate this statement. Include arguments for and against, examples from Christian teachings, and a conclusion. [12]

Christianity & Catholic Christianity	# Different Forms of Worship

Worship is a Christian's way of expressing their **love** of, **respect** for, and **devotion** to God.

Christian denominations have different forms of worship

- For Christians, Sunday is the '**Lord's Day**', when they celebrate the **Sabbath**. Most churches have their main service on a **Sunday morning**.
- Worship often includes prayers, readings from the Bible, a sermon and the Eucharist (see p.14) — the different denominations place varying amounts of **importance** on each, creating **differences** in worship.

> **Sabbath**
> *the holy day of rest*

> If you're studying Catholic Christianity, just read the relevant column of the table below.

Some worship is liturgical

- '**Liturgical**' means that services follow a set pattern written out by the Church.

	Anglican Worship	Catholic Worship	Orthodox Worship
OVERVIEW	• Sunday morning services **usually** include the Eucharist. • Worship is guided by the '**Common Worship**' book, based on the Book of Common Prayer from 1662.	• Sunday morning services **always** include the Eucharist. • Catholics call the Eucharist '**Mass**'. • The '**Roman Missal**' sets out the contents of the service.	• The main Sunday service is the '**Divine Liturgy**', which centres on the Eucharist. • The service is usually based on the liturgy of St John Chrysostom.
THE SERVICE	• A **confession** of sin and a request for God's mercy is said by everyone. [This is called the '**penitential rite**' by Catholics.] • There are readings (including one **gospel** reading) and a sermon — this part is known as the '**liturgy of the Word**'. The **Nicene** or **Apostle's Creed** is then recited. • The priest says prayers over bread and wine — this is called the '**liturgy of the Eucharist**'. • Then the congregation says the **Lord's Prayer** (see p.16) and 'shares the peace' by shaking hands. They receive the bread and wine. [Catholics call this the '**rite of Communion**'.]		• Services contain similar elements to Anglican and Catholic ones — a sermon, Bible readings, the Nicene Creed and blessing of bread and wine. • They include the '**Litany**', where the priest says prayers and the congregation responds with 'Lord have mercy'. Worshippers sing or chant for most of the service. • Services are often longer than most Anglican and Catholic services, and people stand for the majority of the time.

- For many, public worship helps them to feel involved in a wider Christian community.
- It can also help them feel closer to Jesus, as they believe he is there in the church with them.
- Following traditions also helps Christians to feel connected to other worshippers throughout history.

> "For where two or three gather in my name, there am I with them."
> *Matthew 18:20 NIV*

Different Forms of Worship

Other worship is non-liturgical

- The worship of the Society of Friends (Quakers) is non-liturgical, and it is usually unstructured.
- Worshippers sit together in silence, but they are free to pray or speak out loud.

- **Methodist** services **don't** have to follow a set structure, but there is a 'Methodist Worship Book' with suggested liturgy for parts of worship, e.g. the **Eucharist**.
- Services feature **hymns**, **readings**, a **sermon** and **prayers**. The **Eucharist** also takes place, but **not every week**.

- Worship in Evangelical Churches (e.g. Pentecostals) is often spontaneous. Worshippers believe they're inspired by the Spirit — this is called 'charismatic worship'.
- It might inspire them to pray, clap, dance or shout. Sometimes they 'speak in tongues' — praying in an unrecognisable language.

Some Christians prefer the **freedom** of worshipping God in a **less structured** way. Others view non-liturgical worship as **unsuitable** for the level of **respect** that religious services require.

Some Christians also engage in private worship

- Many Christians worship informally at home (not just on Sundays). This can be anything from saying grace before a meal to singing worship songs with family, to reading the Bible or praying (see p.16).
- Lots of Christians worship both publicly and privately — private worship can help them keep God in mind throughout their everyday lives. Some also find greater freedom in private worship — they decide how they worship God and so feel a better connection with God.

EXAM QUESTION

Who's singing out of tune? Hymn...
Give two reasons why some Christians might prefer liturgical worship. [2]

The Sacraments

Sacraments play a key role in **worship** and **belief** for many Christians.

Different denominations believe in different sacraments

- Roman Catholic and Orthodox Churches believe in **seven sacraments** (see p.15), but most Protestants accept only **baptism** and the **Eucharist** as sacraments — they believe only these two were **prescribed** by Jesus in the **Gospels**.   Many believe that the sacraments bring people **closer to God**.

- Quakers and the Salvation Army don't celebrate the Eucharist or any other sacraments, seeing them as **unnecessary symbols** for the inward acceptance of God's grace.

> **sacrament**
> *a ceremony (usually carried out by a minister or priest) through which Christians believe they receive God's grace — it is a sign of God's grace working within them*

Baptism is an important sacrament for many Christians

- Baptism is seen as a sacrament because Jesus was baptised. After his resurrection, he told his disciples to go out and baptise people.

- Baptism makes someone a member of God's family and welcomes them to the Church. Some Christians believe that baptising cleanses people from the original sin that everyone is born with.

- Babies are baptised in many denominations, e.g. Anglican, Catholic and Methodist. (They will also baptise adults if they weren't baptised as children and want to join the Church.)

> **"...go and make disciples of all nations, baptising them in the name of the Father and of the Son and of the Holy Spirit"** *Matthew 28:19 NIV*

> **"no one can enter the kingdom of God unless they are born of water and the Spirit"** *John 3:5 NIV*

A sign of the cross is made on the baby, and in many Churches holy water is poured three times over the forehead (in the name of the Father, Son and Holy Spirit). Orthodox Christians baptise babies by total immersion.	Denominations that baptise babies also usually have confirmation — a person 'confirms' their faith when they reach an age that they can declare it themselves.	But some denominations — for example Baptists and Pentecostals — believe you shouldn't be baptised until you're old enough to accept Christianity for yourself. They hold believers' baptisms, when adults who wish to join the Church are baptised by total immersion.

There are many different understandings of the Eucharist

The **Eucharist** is where Christians remember the **Last Supper** (see p.10) with **bread and wine**. Many denominations see it as a **sacrament**, but have **different beliefs** about the bread and wine, and transubstantiation:

> **transubstantiation**
> *the idea that the bread and wine used become the flesh and blood of Christ*

Catholics believe in **transubstantiation** and every Mass is a re-enactment of Christ's sacrifice (see p.10). They believe that they receive the **saving power** of Jesus into themselves through the bread and wine.	**Lutherans, Methodists** and most **Anglicans** believe Holy Communion is more than just an 'intellectual' commemoration of the Last Supper — it's a re-enactment. They believe that there is a 'real presence' of Christ in the bread and wine, but they don't believe that transubstantiation occurs. **"Transubstantiation... in the Supper of the Lord, cannot be proved by holy Writ..."** *39 Articles XXVIII*	Baptists view the bread and wine as **symbols**, but believe that God is **present** through the act of Christians **coming together** to share Communion. The **bread** and **non-alcoholic wine** are set out on a simple **table**. The **bread** is later **offered** from person to person, and the **wine** drunk from small **individual** cups.

Denominations which place **more meaning** on the bread and wine (e.g. Catholicism and Orthodox) hold Eucharists **more often** — they believe it's essential for sustaining their **relationship** with God. They tend to use a more ornate table (an **altar**), and have more **ritual** surrounding the Eucharist (e.g. using **incense**). **Catholics** will be given bread by the priest and drink wine from a **shared cup**. Orthodox Christians are given the bread and wine **together** on a special **spoon**.

Immerse yourself and learn all about baptism...

Close the book and jot down the different denominations' beliefs about baptism and the Eucharist.

The Sacraments

Catholics believe there are **seven** specific sacraments through which God can communicate his **grace** directly. Some see the **whole world** as **sacramental** — they can experience **God's grace** through his creation.

The seven sacraments — God shows his grace

> "The seven sacraments touch all the stages and all the important moments of Christian life..." *Catechism of the Catholic Church, 1210*

① BAPTISM

This marks a person's official entry into the Church (see p.14).

② CONFIRMATION

In this ceremony, a Christian (often a teenager) renews the vows made on their behalf at baptism. **Confirmation** is believed to strengthen the ties of the confirmed to the Church and to God. In Catholic confirmations, the bishop anoints the believer's forehead with holy oil called chrism.

③ RECONCILIATION

This involves confession of a sin, following by contrition, penance and absolution. This is how Catholics seek to obtain forgiveness for the sins they commit. They must tell a priest about any sinful things that they've done. The priest will give a penance (a certain number of prayers to be said, or an action to be done) and will then pronounce absolution (God's forgiveness).

④ ANOINTING THE SICK

A priest or bishop anoints a seriously unwell person with the oil of the sick. Catholics believe that, through this, the Holy Spirit renews the person's faith and strength to cope with their illness and accept their suffering. The anointing is also believed to link the person's suffering to Christ's suffering, allow their sins to be forgiven and to heal them, if that is God's will.

⑤ MATRIMONY

Catholics believe Jesus performed his first miracle at a wedding. They believe that God is present at the ceremony and promises are made before him — couples joined in Holy Matrimony should be together for life. As it's a sacrament, the union is a way that God blesses the couple, and he also blesses them through one another.

⑥ HOLY ORDERS

This is the process by which men are ordained as deacons, priests or bishops. Like matrimony, it is a commitment that they make for life.

⑦ EUCHARIST

The Eucharist (Mass) is seen as *"the source and summit of the Christian life"* (Catechism of the Catholic Church 1324). Receiving the body and blood of Christ (see p.14) joins people together in their faith and gives them the strength to live Christian lives and face any problems they may encounter.

> "...in the breaking of the Eucharistic bread, we are taken up into communion with Him and with one another." *Lumen gentium Chapter 1 Paragraph 7:53*

Some of the bread and wine that is blessed but not consumed is kept in the church — people believe Jesus is still present in it, and focus on it as they pray and express their love for Jesus. This is known as 'eucharistic adoration'.

Catholic funerals have three parts

The funeral rite isn't a sacrament, but it's important.

- The **Vigil of Prayer** takes place the day before the funeral and is sometimes held at home. Readings and prayers form the service, which aims to **help** family and friends prepare to say **goodbye**.
- Attending a funeral allows Catholics to join together in **praying** to God to **take care** of the person.

The **Funeral Liturgy** often includes Holy Communion (the 'Requiem Mass'). Its purpose is to pray for the soul of the dead person.	The coffin is covered with a white cloth (a **pall**) as it is carried into the church.	The coffin is sprinkled with **holy water** and the priest says, "In the waters of baptism [name] died with Christ, and rose with him to new life. May s/he now share with him in eternal glory."	The coffin is later sprinkled again and perfumed with **incense**. The **Paschal candle** sits beside it.

- The **Committal** is a short ceremony that happens at the **cemetery** (or the **crematorium** if the person wished to be cremated). The priest says "ashes to ashes, dust to dust" as the body goes back to the **earth**.

REVISION TASK

Big Cats Rarely Ask Me 'Ham or Egg?'...

...is a good way to remember the first letters of the sacraments. Try summarising each sacrament in one or two sentences <u>in your own words</u> — make sure you know why each one is important.

Prayer and Pilgrimage

Prayer and pilgrimage are both ways in which Christians might **strengthen** their **relationship** with God.

Prayer puts people in touch with their God

> "Prayer is the raising of one's mind and heart to God"
> *Catechism of the Catholic Church 2559*

- **Prayer** is when believers mentally or vocally **communicate** with God — it should be part of **daily life**.

- Prayer can come in many **different forms**:

Thanksgiving — thanking God

Adoration — worshipping God

Confession — admitting your sins

Supplication — asking God for something

Intercession — asking God to help other people

- Believers draw **comfort** from the fact that God is listening to them. They also listen for what **he** is saying to **them** — many believe prayer helps them to **find out** what God wants them to do in **life**.

Formal prayer

- Most denominations have **formal**, set prayers that are Church tradition — they can be said during acts of worship in church, and also in private.

- The Lord's Prayer is very important. It's based on the words Jesus used when he told his disciples how to pray. It covers key themes — e.g. the idea that God is 'Our Father' and he provides for people's physical needs.

> "This, then, is how you should pray: 'Our Father in heaven, hallowed be your name, your kingdom come, your will be done, on earth as it is in heaven. Give us today our daily bread. And forgive us our debts, as we also have forgiven our debtors. And lead us not into temptation, but deliver us from the evil one.' " *Matthew 6:9-13 NIV*

Informal prayer

- **Informal prayers** are where the individual talks to God in their **own words**. They're sometimes called '**extempore**' prayers, and can be used in worship and privately.

- Informal prayers are more **personal** and show the individual's **connection** with God — many Christians **prefer** them to set prayers.

Catholics have different forms of popular piety

You only need to read this bit if you're studying Catholic Christianity.

- Catholics use the **Rosary** when praying. The **cross** is **held** when reciting the Apostles' Creed, and prayers are said as the **beads** are **moved** through the fingers, e.g. Ave Maria (Hail Mary). The beads represent the **key events** in Christianity (known as **mysteries**), such as the birth, death and resurrection of Jesus — the rosary helps people **think** about these while praying.

- The '**Stations of the Cross**' are pictures in church of Jesus's **suffering** — Catholics use them as a **focus** for **contemplation** on these events.

- Some **disagree** with these forms of 'popular piety'. Some Protestants think the rosary encourages prayers to be repeated **without** giving **thought** to the words themselves.

- Many Protestants wouldn't say the **Hail Mary** prayer, as most **don't** believe in praying to **Mary**.

- Some people might argue that praying while focusing on the Stations of the Cross creates a **danger** of **worshipping idols**.

Prayer and Pilgrimage

Pilgrimages can help believers feel nearer to God

- Pilgrimages aren't compulsory in Christianity, but many see them as important.
  Luke 2:41-43 tells the story of the pilgrimage Jesus and his parents made to Jerusalem.

> **"Pilgrimages evoke our earthly journey toward heaven..."**
> *Catechism of the Catholic Church 2691*

- Christians make pilgrimages for a variety of reasons:

| to seek healing | to seek forgiveness | to connect to God | to deepen their faith | to escape normal life | to concentrate more on religion |

- Pilgrims can also learn from each other. The journey reflects the path they're trying to follow towards God.

There are various places Christians might visit

- People may visit places that are significant in Christianity. For example:

Jerusalem ⟹ Christians can visit key places in Jesus's life and death here.

Rome ⟹ Roman Catholics often visit Rome because it is the home of the Pope.

- Some Christians, especially Catholics, make pilgrimages to shrines where Mary has appeared.
- These include Walsingham (popular with some Anglicans as well as Catholics) and Lourdes.
- Catholics also visit shrines to saints.

LOURDES

- The water in Lourdes is said to have healing properties which can cure ill health.
- Lots of people believe miracles take place there.
- Some Christians see shrines such as Lourdes as being too commercialised, with too many people.

Protestants are more likely to visit places they can find peace to study the Bible and pray.
For example:
- the quiet island of Iona (which has a long history of Christianity)
- Taizé, where they can join worship at the monastery.

- Some Christians regard pilgrimage as unnecessary — they believe that the journey inside is what matters.

EXAM TIP

I make a daily pilgrimage to the biscuit tin...

Make sure you know why people go on pilgrimages and the differences between the famous Christian pilgrimage sites, e.g. some are famous for visions, others for events that happened there.

Christianity	# Christmas and Easter

Christmas and Easter are the two most important celebrations in the Christian calendar.

Christmas *is a celebration of Jesus's birth*

Christmas celebrates how Jesus was born in **Bethlehem** — there he was worshipped by **shepherds** after an **angel** told them that *"a Saviour has been born to you; he is the Messiah, the Lord"* (Luke 2:11 NIV).

Christmas is celebrated by most Christians on **25th December**, but for **Orthodox** Christians it's **7th January**.

- Christmas comes after a period called **Advent**, which begins four Sundays before Christmas.
- Advent is significant for many Christians as it's time they spend **getting ready** to celebrate **Jesus's birth** — a time for **prayer** and **reflection**.
- **Advent candles** are lit in homes and churches, and children may use **Advent calendars** to count off the days until Christmas.

- Lots of Roman Catholic, Orthodox and Anglican churches have a '**Midnight Mass**' to welcome Christmas Day, and most Christians go to church on **Christmas morning** to **celebrate**.
- Many churches hold services in the days **after Christmas**, carrying on to **Epiphany** (6th January) — the day that the **Magi** (wise men) went to see Jesus in Bethlehem.

Customs **vary** around the world. **Gifts** are exchanged to symbolise the fact that Jesus was **God's gift** to the world, and to remember how the Magi *"presented him with gifts of gold, frankincense and myrrh"* (Matthew 2:11 NIV).

- Some Christians dislike modern Christmas **traditions** and **customs**, e.g. **Santa Claus** (Father Christmas), giving **expensive presents**, and **excessive eating** and **drinking**.
- They believe that some of these modern traditions **devalue** the **true meaning** of Christmas. Others feel that it has retained too much **pagan** influence, such as Christmas trees.

Christmas and Easter 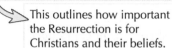 Christianity

Easter celebrates Jesus's resurrection

- Easter is the most **important** festival for Christians, since it celebrates **Jesus's victory** over death, when God raised him **back to life** after his crucifixion (see p.10).

- This reminds people that God **loves** them so much that he was **willing** to suffer death on the cross, and this gives them hope of **eternal life**.

> **"And if Christ has not been raised, our preaching is useless and so is your faith"**
> *1 Corinthians 15:14*

This outlines how important the Resurrection is for Christians and their beliefs.

LENT
- **Lent** is the **40 days** before Easter.
- On **Ash Wednesday** (the first day of Lent), ash is put on believers' **foreheads** to show they're sorry for their **sins**.
- Some Christians **fast** (**eat less** and have only **simple food**) during Lent to mark when Jesus fasted for 40 days in the desert. They **stop fasting** on **Easter Sunday**.

- The lead-up to **Easter Day**, the day of resurrection, is marked by a number of important events:

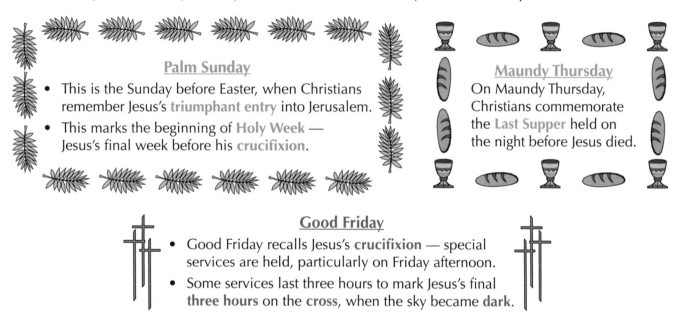

Palm Sunday
- This is the Sunday before Easter, when Christians remember Jesus's **triumphant entry** into Jerusalem.
- This marks the beginning of **Holy Week** — Jesus's final week before his **crucifixion**.

Maundy Thursday
On Maundy Thursday, Christians commemorate the **Last Supper** held on the night before Jesus died.

Good Friday
- Good Friday recalls Jesus's **crucifixion** — special services are held, particularly on Friday afternoon.
- Some services last three hours to mark Jesus's final **three hours** on the **cross**, when the sky became **dark**.

- **Easter Day** is a **joyous** occasion, when Jesus's resurrection is celebrated:

- Some churches hold services on the Saturday night, and most have **special services** on the Sunday morning.
- The **Paschal candle** is lit during services in Anglican and Catholic churches. Worshippers light their own candle from its flame, which represents Jesus as the **Light of the World**.
- Some churches hold **sunrise services** to remember how Mary Magdalene discovered at daybreak that Jesus's tomb was empty. The rising of the **sun** is symbolic of **God's Son** rising from the dead.
- **Eggs** are associated with Easter as a symbol of **new life**.
  - However, some view chocolate Easter eggs as **commercialisation** of the festival.

Learning about Easter is an eggcellent way to gain marks...

Working from Lent to Easter Sunday, draw a timeline of Christian Easter celebrations. Next to each day, scribble down what happens and then check your answers against this page.

Beliefs, Teachings and Practices — Christianity & Catholic Christianity

The Work of the Church

Churches aren't just about holding services. They're active in the **local community** too.

Churches play an *important role* in the *local community*

Most communities in the UK have access to at least one church. The role of the local church is to put the **Christian faith into action** — this includes **caring** for the community, as seen in lots of Christian teaching:

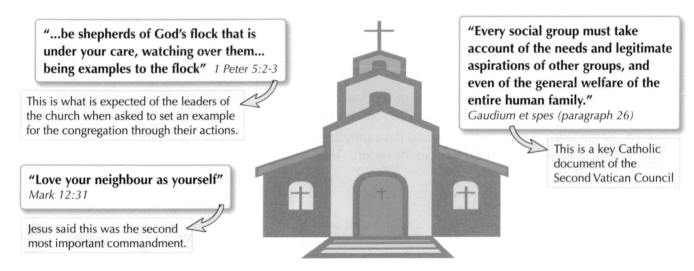

"...be shepherds of God's flock that is under your care, watching over them... being examples to the flock" *1 Peter 5:2-3*

This is what is expected of the leaders of the church when asked to set an example for the congregation through their actions.

"Every social group must take account of the needs and legitimate aspirations of other groups, and even of the general welfare of the entire human family." *Gaudium et spes (paragraph 26)*

This is a key Catholic document of the Second Vatican Council

"Love your neighbour as yourself" *Mark 12:31*

Jesus said this was the second most important commandment.

Churches put this into practice in many **different ways**:

 By providing regular **services** and a place for **quiet reflection** — most churches hold a Sunday service and may also have other acts of worship throughout the week.

 By providing **rites of passage** such as baptisms, confirmations, weddings and funerals (p.14-15).

 By running **youth groups** and Sunday Schools to engage young people in the local community.

 By offering **support** and **advice** to people in need — e.g. visiting and praying for people in hospital.

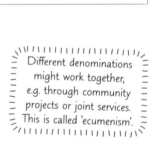 Different denominations might work together, e.g. through community projects or joint services. This is called 'ecumenism'.

 Some churchgoers work as **Street Pastors** — they volunteer in towns and cities on **Friday** and **Saturday nights** to support anyone in need of help. This demonstrates Christian love.

 Some **foodbanks** in the UK are run by churches. People **donate** food which the foodbank then **distributes** to those who need it the most.

 Many churches also raise money for **charity**.

 EXAM QUESTION

It's my mission to get you to learn this page...

Give two examples of the work that churches do in their local communities. [2]

Beliefs, Teachings and Practices — Christianity & Catholic Christianity

The Work of the Church

Evangelism tells people about Christianity

- In Mark 16:15, Jesus told his disciples to *"Go into all the world and preach the gospel to all creation"* (NIV). Many Christians believe that they should be prepared to do the same.

  evangelism
  spreading the Christian message with the aim of converting people

  > **"As the Father has sent me, I am sending you."** *John 20:21 NIV*

- They believe that by evangelising they can help people **discover** their **real purpose** in life and find **salvation**. They feel **excited** to tell other people about **Jesus's love**.

   Pope Francis said *"The primary reason for evangelizing is the love of Jesus which we have received..."* (Evangelii Gaudium 264).

- For some, evangelism is about telling people **directly** about God. This can sometimes cause problems — people may feel **offended**. Others try to **demonstrate** God's love through their actions, to bring people **closer** to God.

- Here are a few different types of evangelism:

Gideons distribute copies of the **Bible** in places like hotels and care homes.	Churches might ask the congregation to **bring** along a **friend** who wouldn't normally go to church.	The **Salvation Army** helps people by providing **hot meals** and **beds** for homeless people. They also attend **emergencies**, such as floods.

- As church attendance falls, evangelism is increasingly important. The Church of England and Church in Wales are finding ways to interest **new people** in churches that **don't** follow the **traditional model** — for example worshipping in alternative venues like **cafés**, or creating a café **atmosphere** in church. Through initiatives called '**Fresh Expressions**' and '**Pioneer Ministry**', they offer a new approach for modern society.

- **Missionaries** spread the Christian message **abroad**. Many aren't there to preach, but to use their **skills** to help **disadvantaged people** — e.g. a doctor might choose to work in a poor country. These people demonstrate the message of Christianity through their **actions**.

Reconciliation works towards peace and unity

- Christians believe in justice — all people are equal in God's eyes, so they should be treated fairly. Christian organisations help people being treated unfairly due to war, religious persecution or poverty.

- In Matthew 5:9 Jesus said *"Blessed are the peacemakers"* (NIV). Christians believe that reconciliation (coming together and making peace) is needed between people who have been in conflict with one another — just as Jesus brought God and humankind together through the atonement (p.11).

- These are two examples of organisations that work for reconciliation:

The Corrymeela Community	Pax Christi
• The **Corrymeela Community** in Northern Ireland was founded to help **heal** the country's political and religious **divisions**. • It works with people in areas where there is **tension** and strives to help people **understand** each other and **reconcile** through group activities and discussions.	• **Pax Christi** is an international **Catholic** organisation working for **human rights**, **disarmament** and **peace**. • They believe **violence** should be **avoided**, and they work to create a world where people can live in **harmony**.

The Work of the Church

Organisations and churches help persecuted Christians

- Millions around the world **suffer** for being Christians — some endure **prison sentences** or even **death**.
- Organisations give support by providing **Bibles** so people can continue worshipping in secret. They offer **training** to church members and **support** people who have lost their homes.
- Churches **pray** for the persecuted and may send **money**. Christians might **petition** for **government** help.

Christian charities help those in need

- In the story of the **sheep** and **goats** (Matthew 25:31-46), Jesus explains that people who have been **good** (the sheep) and have helped others will be **looked after** by God. People who **haven't** (the goats) will **suffer**. The story tells Christians that they are **helping Jesus** when they help others.

- Because of this, **charity** is very important to many Christians. But it's **not** all about giving **money** — it must be done with **love**. In 1 Corinthians 13:3, St Paul said *"If I give all I possess to the poor... but do not have love, I gain nothing"* (NIV).

Christian Aid works **globally** to relieve poverty. They set up projects in the developing world, drawing on the skills of **local people**. The organisation also aims to change **government policy** to help reduce the suffering of the world's poor, e.g. through **debt relief**, and **fair-trade** products.

CAFOD (Catholic Agency for Overseas Development) works to fight **poverty** and **injustice** around the world. They work through churches, helping in **emergencies**, but also giving people the **skills** to help themselves.

Tearfund is an **evangelical** organisation — it helps communities with projects run **through** their **churches**. Their work includes trying to end **hunger**, resolving **tension** in conflict zones and helping **refugees**. They also help areas hit by **natural disasters**.

Christian Aid and CAFOD believe in **development** — 'helping people to help themselves', **whatever** their faith.

There are many Catholic charities

This section is only for people studying Catholic Christianity.

Evangelii Gaudium (187) says that Catholics should strive to **help** the poor *"to be fully a part of society"*. **CAFOD** (see above) is a Roman Catholic organisation, and there are many others that help those in need:

Trócaire → **Trócaire**, part of the Irish Catholic Church, **provides aid** abroad. They help people **escape poverty**, but also help in **emergencies**.

SVP → The **St Vincent de Paul Society** (SVP) helps people in **poverty**. They provide support by **visiting** the isolated and ill, helping them with **daily tasks**, providing **schemes** and **clubs** to help the disabled, and **donating food** to the homeless.

Missio → **Missio** is an organisation that **supports churches** abroad that are **struggling** to fund themselves, e.g. by **training** church leaders. It also runs projects to provide **education** and **healthcare** for children living in poverty.

Sheep — good, goats — baaaad...

In the exam, some of the 4 mark questions will ask you how a particular belief influences the people of a religion. You'll have to describe two ways in detail in order to get full marks.

Revision Summary

That was a lot to take in there, so now see how you get on with these exam-style questions. Answer 1-12 if you're studying Christianity. If you're studying Catholic Christianity, answer them all except 4 and 5. If there's anything you can't answer, go back through the section and have another go when you've re-read it.

Christianity and Catholic Christianity

Let's get cracking — have a go at these 1 mark multiple choice questions.

1) Which of the following words means that God is all-powerful?
a) just   b) omnipotent   c) immanent   d) benevolent

2) Which of the following is Jesus's return to heaven to be with God the Father?
a) resurrection   b) Last Supper   c) ascension   d) crucifixion

You've found your feet now, so let's jump up to 2 marks. Make two brief points to scoop both the marks.

3) Give two beliefs about the Last Judgement.

4) Give two examples of different types of evil. ⟵   *Only answer these questions if you're studying Christianity.*

5) Give two ways that Christians celebrate Easter. ⟵

For the 4 mark questions, you need to give two points and develop them to get full marks.

6) Explain two contrasting Christian views about the creation story.

7) Explain two ways in which belief in salvation influences Christians today.

8) Explain two contrasting Christian views on the Eucharist.

Organise your points and write concisely in the 4 and 5 mark questions — make your points clearly.

All the way up to 5 marks now. Explain your points and make sure you refer to a sacred text.

9) Explain two Christian teachings about the Trinity.

10) Explain two beliefs that Christians hold about Jesus's resurrection.

11) Explain two reasons why evangelism is important to Christians.

Turn to the 'Do Well in Your Exam' section for tips on writing essays.

Now it's the one you've been looking forward to — the 12 mark question.
You'll get a list of things that you've got to have in your answer, which is handy for creating a plan.
You'll be asked to give arguments for and against a statement, so be sure to include plenty of detail.

12) 'Pilgrimage is the best way for a Christian to develop their relationship with God.'
Evaluate this statement. Your answer should include the following:

- examples from Christian teachings
- arguments that support the statement
- arguments that disagree with the statement
- a conclusion

Catholic Christianity

13) Which of the following is not part of the Catholic funeral rite? [1]
a) Reconciliation   b) Committal   c) Requiem Mass   d) Vigil of Prayer

14) Give two beliefs that Catholics hold about purgatory. [2]

15) Explain two contrasting Christian views about the Rosary. [4]

16) Explain two reasons why Catholics believe it's important to 'love your neighbour'.
You should refer to religious teaching or sacred texts. [5]

17) 'The sacraments are the most important part of a Catholic's faith.' ⟵   *There are an extra 3 marks for SPaG for this question, so check your writing carefully.*
Evaluate this statement. Your answer should include the following:

- examples from Catholic teachings
- arguments that support the statement
- arguments that disagree with the statement
- a conclusion. [12]

Beliefs, Teachings and Practices — Christianity & Catholic Christianity

| Islam | # Introduction to Islam |

Islam was founded in the **7th century**. It **shares** some ideas with **Christianity**. Muslims believe in **one god**, **Allah**. The **Qur'an** is the Muslim **holy book** — Muslims also follow the prophet **Muhammad**'s teaching.

Islam *is divided into* two main traditions — *Sunni and Shi'a*

- About **85-90%** of Muslims are **Sunni** Muslims — most of the rest are **Shi'a** Muslims.
- Muhammad was the **founder** of Islam — Allah revealed the **Qur'an** to him. After Muhammad **died**, Muslims had to choose a **new leader** (caliph). The **next four caliphs** were Abu Bakr, Umar, Uthman and Ali.

- Some Muslims had wanted **Ali** to be the **first** caliph, and thought the first **three** caliphs shouldn't have been given the role.

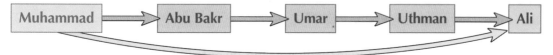

- Others Muslims said Ali **shouldn't** be the caliph at all.

- After Ali died, **two** groups formed — the **Sunnis** and the **Shi'as**. Each group followed a different **line** of caliphs:

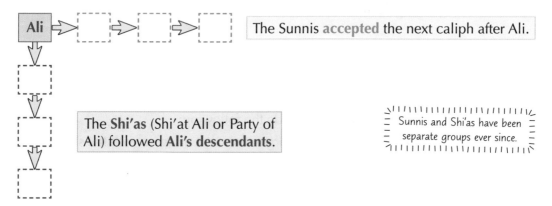

The Sunnis **accepted** the next caliph after Ali.

The **Shi'as** (Shi'at Ali or Party of Ali) followed **Ali's descendants**.

Sunnis and Shi'as have been separate groups ever since.

Sunnis *and* Shi'as *have many* similar beliefs

- Sunnis and Shi'as **share many beliefs**, but have some **different ideas**.

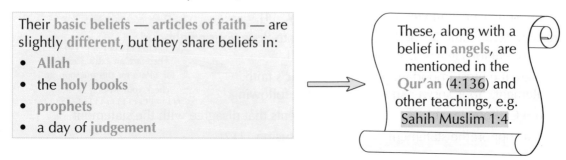

Their **basic beliefs** — **articles of faith** — are slightly **different**, but they share beliefs in:
- **Allah**
- the **holy books**
- **prophets**
- a day of **judgement**

These, along with a belief in **angels**, are mentioned in the **Qur'an** (4:136) and other teachings, e.g. Sahih Muslim 1:4.

Key Sunni beliefs

- **No one** after Muhammad received **knowledge** from **Allah**. Muslims should **focus** on **Muhammad** and his way of life (**sunnah** — see p.29) rather than paying too much attention to **Ali** and his **sons**.
- Muslims should be guided by the **consensus** (majority view) of the **community**.

There are six articles of faith in Sunni Islam:

① belief that Allah is the **one** and **only god** (Tawhid)

② belief in **angels** (Malaikah)

③ belief in the **holy books**

④ belief in Allah's **prophets** (Nubuwwah)

⑤ belief in the **Day of Judgement**

⑥ belief that Allah knows and decides everything that's going to happen (**predestination — al-Qadr**)

Key Shi'a beliefs

- **Ali** was the first **true** caliph. **Allah** gave him **knowledge** to ensure his teaching and actions were **right**.

There are five articles of faith in Shi'a Islam

They're known as the **Usul ad-Din** — **foundations** of faith:

① belief that Allah is the **one** and **only god** (Tawhid)

② belief in **divine justice** (Adalat)

③ belief in **prophethood** (Nubuwwah)

④ belief in the authority of **imams** (Imamah)

⑤ belief in the **Day of Resurrection** (Ma'ad)

- There are **many branches** of Shi'a Islam. They share a common belief in a **line of imams** after **Ali**, who all had the same **knowledge** from Allah as Ali. The different **branches** of Shi'a Islam split off from each other after **disagreements** about the **line** of imams.
- The **Twelvers** are the **largest** branch, but there are many others:

IMAMS
- Shi'a imams are **leaders** and **figureheads** of the religion. They're all **descendants** of Muhammad.
- In **Sunni** Islam, the word '**imam**' simply means '**prayer leader**'.

12 **Twelver** Shi'as believe in a line of **12** imams, the **last** of whom is in **hiding** and will eventually **return**. The Twelvers are led by **religious scholars** while they wait for the last imam's return.

7 **Isma'ili** Shi'as (often called '**Seveners**') thought the **seventh** imam should be **Isma'il**, the **elder brother** of the one chosen by the Twelvers. The biggest group of Isma'ilis today, the **Nizaris**, think each imam can **select** the next and are still led by an imam now, known as the **Aga Khan**.

Seveners, Twelvers — sounds like maths, not RS...

As a quick task to keep you on your toes — shut this book, grab a piece of paper and see if you can write down the articles of faith for Sunni and Shi'a Islam.

Key Beliefs in Islam

Islam is a **monotheistic** religion — Muslims believe in only **one god**, **Allah**. They believe in many **prophets**.

Tawhid *is central to Islam*

- The word **Allah** is from the Arabic **al-ilah**, meaning '**the god**', i.e. the **only** god. Several of the **ninety-nine names** of Allah (see below) make this clear, including **al-Ahad** (the one and only) and **al-Wahid** (the one).

  > "Say, 'He is Allah, [who is] One.' " *Qur'an 112:1*

- Saying Allah is the **only god** is the first part of the **shahadah**, the Muslim **declaration of faith** (see p.31).

- **Shirk** is seen as the **worst sin**.
  (**Images** of Muhammad aren't allowed, in case of **shirk**.)
  Muslims therefore disagree with the **Christian** idea of the **Holy Trinity** (see p.3) and **polytheism**.

  shirk
  believing in other gods as well as Allah, or that anyone or anything could share in Allah's oneness

  polytheism
  believing in multiple gods

  > "Allah does not forgive association with Him, but He forgives what is less than that..." *Qur'an 4:116*

  'Association with Him' is worshipping other gods as well as Allah.

- According to a **hadith** (see p.29), **Muhammad** said that when telling **non-Muslims** about Islam, the **first thing** Muslims should mention is **Tawhid**.

  > "let the first thing to which you will invite them, be the Tauhid [Tawhid] of Allah." *Sahih al-Bukhari 93:469*

Allah *has many characteristics*

MERCIFUL — Muslims believe Allah shows **mercy** and **compassion**. **All but one** of the Qur'an's chapters **begin** by saying this — it's known as the **bismillah**. They believe Allah is **kind** and **forgives** people's **sins**.

> "In the name of Allah, the Entirely Merciful, the Especially Merciful" *Qur'an 1:1*

OMNIPOTENT — Allah is **all-powerful**. He **created** the **universe** and is in **control** of everything. He has **predetermined** people's lives (decided **what will happen**), though people do have **free will** (see p.30).

BENEVOLENT — Allah is **all-good** — he can do no evil. He **cares** for his people — this is seen in his **intervention** in the world, e.g. his **revelations** to the prophets were to show people how to live a **good life**.

JUST — Muslims believe Allah will **judge** people's behaviour in a **fair way**. This concept is particularly **important** to **Shi'a** Muslims — known as **Adalat**, it's one of the **Usul ad-Din** (see p.25).

IMMANENT — Allah is **present** and **involved** in the world. He's **close** to every human and **knows** them.

> "And We have already created man and know what his soul whispers to him, and We are closer to him than [his] jugular vein." *Qur'an 50:16*

TRANSCENDENT — Allah's also **above everything** — he can't be thought of in **human** terms. He has **no equal**.

There are **ninety-nine names** for Allah listed in the Qur'an. Each refers to one of his **characteristics**. The first four characteristics given above are **each** English translations of one of these names (originally in **Arabic**). Muslims recite them in **daily prayers**.

Key Beliefs in Islam

There are many prophets in Islam

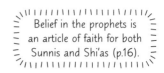

Belief in the prophets is an article of faith for both Sunnis and Shi'as (p.16).

- Allah's **compassion** means he can't leave people to **sin** without **helping** them. So he sends **messages** about how to live a **good** life. He almost always does this via **angels**, who pass on his words to human **prophets** (**rasuls**). **Risalah** is the concept of **messengership** — the way Allah **communicates** with **humans**.

- Allah **chose** many people as **prophets**. **25** prophets are mentioned in the **Qur'an**, although some believe there have been **124 000**. Some prophets were given **holy books** to pass on to humankind.

- Muslims believe the prophets taught the **same basic ideas**, most importantly belief in **one god**. They see all the prophets as **equal** to each other.

> **"We make no distinction between any of them"** *Qur'an 2:136*

- Muslims believe the **prophets** performed **miracles** — they did so to **prove** they were really prophets.

- The first prophet was **Adam**, who was also the **first man**, created by Allah in his image. Others were **Ibrahim** (Abraham), **Isma'il** (Ishmael), **Musa** (Moses), **Dawud** (David) and **Isa** (Jesus):

Adam	Adam was sent to **Earth** after eating fruit **forbidden** to him by Allah. Allah **forgave** him his sin though. Adam is considered to have been the first **Muslim**. Some believe he first built the **Ka'aba** (p.34).
Ibrahim	Ibrahim **rejected** the idea of **many different** gods and was a **holy** man. He proved his **faith** by being willing to **sacrifice** his own son, **Isma'il** (see p.35). Ibrahim is thought to have rebuilt the **Ka'aba** and he and his family's story plays an **important role** in the **hajj** rituals (see p.34).
Isma'il	Ibrahim's son Isma'il was also a prophet and helped him build the **Ka'aba**. It's believed many Arabs, including **Muhammad**, are **descended** from Isma'il — he's known as **Abul Arab**, the father of the **Arabs**.
Musa	Musa is the **only prophet** that Allah spoke to **directly**, rather than through the angel **Jibril** (Gabriel). He's **important** as he kept trying to guide people to believing in **one god**, even when they worshipped **others**.
Dawud	Dawud is known for **killing Jalut** (Goliath) during a battle between **Jalut's** large army and **Talut's** (Saul's) smaller one. Dawud later succeeded Talut as **king**. As well as his bravery, he's known for his **wisdom** and his **loyalty** to Allah — he would **pray** for a **third** of each night.
Isa	Allah sent Isa when he thought people had **strayed** from **Musa's** teachings. Muslims believe Isa **wasn't crucified** (Allah wouldn't let that happen) but after 3 years' teaching Allah brought him up into **heaven**.

- Muslims believe all these **prophets** paved the way for **Muhammad**:

Muhammad	• **Muhammad** was born about **570 CE** in **Makkah** (Mecca). One day, while Muhammad was **meditating**, Allah sent the **angel Jibril** to him with a message. • Muhammad was **scared** at first, but as **Jibril** gradually revealed more and more of the message from Allah, Muhammad began **preaching** this message to **others**. • **Muhammad** is often called the 'seal of the prophets' — most Muslims believe he was the **last** prophet that there will be. He is believed to have been a **wise leader**, who settled disputes and brought different communities **together**. He performed several **miracles**. • As **Muhammad** was Allah's last prophet, Muslims pay **particular attention** to his words and actions. They use them to work out how to live their lives (p.29), as they see him as a **role model**.

The **early** messages received by Muhammad said people should worship **one god**, **Allah**, and that people would be **judged** on their behaviour. Later on, the **revelations** gave more **detail** on **how** Muslims should live their lives. Eventually, this message from Allah was written down as the **Qur'an**. The **Qur'an** is seen by Muslims as a **miracle** — the **final revelation** from Allah.

Key Beliefs in Islam

Angels are Allah's messengers

- The **purpose** of angels is to **follow** Allah's **orders** and **communicate** with humans, often via the **prophets**. In heaven, they **praise** him and **guard** his throne. They **welcome** humans into **paradise**.

> "They exalt [Him] night and day [and] do not slacken." *Qur'an 21:20*

- They're thought to be **genderless**, made of **light** and to have **wings**. They're **immortal** and don't have **free will**, as their role is to obey Allah — they're therefore **incapable** of **sin**. Allah created them **before** humans.

- Some angels **record** people's **good** and **bad deeds** for the **Day of Judgement**. **Guardian** angels **protect** people from **danger** and **evil**. Some think they're the same thing and **recording** angels act as **guardians** too.

> "Our messengers are with them recording" *Qur'an 43:80*

- Belief in angels is an **article of faith** for **Sunnis**, so it's **important**. The thought of a guardian angel can be **comforting** for Muslims. Having an angel recording their deeds can **influence** Muslims to do **good things**.

Angel	Role
Jibril	Jibril (who you might know as Gabriel) is an **important** angel. He revealed Allah's words (the **Qur'an**) to **Muhammad**. He also revealed messages to **other prophets**, so he's known as the angel of **revelation**. He told **Maryam** (Mary) she was pregnant with **Isa** (Jesus) — see Qur'an 19:16-22. "Gabriel ... has brought the Qur'an down upon your heart, [O Muhammad], by permission of Allah." *Qur'an 2:97*
Mika'il	Mika'il (Michael) is also an **important** angel. He asks Allah to **forgive** people's **sins**.
Izrail	Izrail (Azrael) is the angel of **death** (Qur'an 32:11). He takes **souls** from people's bodies when they die.
Israfil	It's believed that Israfil (Raphael) will blow the trumpet on the **Day of Judgement**.

The Qur'an is the word of Allah

> Qur'an is sometimes spelt 'Koran' in English.

- Muslims think the Qur'an is the **most important** holy book. They believe it's a **complete** and **accurate** record of Allah's **exact words** to **Muhammad**:

> "he revealed to His Servant what he revealed. The heart did not lie [about] what it saw." *Qur'an 53:10-11*

The Qur'an allows humans to **know Allah**.

- In the Qur'an, Allah tells Muslims what they **need to know** and how to lead their lives to **please him**. Muslims try to live according to its **guidance**. This helps them be **rewarded** by Allah and get to **Paradise**.

 Many Muslims learn the Qur'an **by heart**. The Qur'an was revealed in **Arabic** — if it's written in another **language** the meaning might **change**, so Muslims learn Arabic to ensure they're reading the **true** Qur'an.

 There's often **dispute** over how to **interpret** the Qur'an though, e.g. in relation to **jihad** (p.34). It can be **difficult** to apply its teachings to **modern life**, because so much has changed since it was revealed.

The Qur'an is divided into 114 Surahs

- The Qur'an is organised into **114 surahs** (**chapters**), each made up of **ayahs** (**verses**). The **surahs** are in **order of length** — **longest first**, **shortest last** (except surah 1, a **short statement** of Muslims' basic beliefs).

- Because the Qur'an is so **important**, Muslims treat it with great **respect**. The Qur'an is often **ornately decorated**, inside and out. Many Muslims:

- keep their Qur'an **wrapped up** to keep it clean
- **wash their hands** before touching it
- keep it on a **higher shelf** than all other books
- place it on a **special stand** when they read it

- The Qur'an is read during private and public **prayers**, so Muslims get to know it well.

Beliefs, Teachings and Practices — Islam

Key Beliefs in Islam

There are other holy books in Islam

As well as the Qur'an, Muslims see the Suhuf Ibrahim, the Tawrat, the Zabur and the Injil as holy books. But they believe they've been changed over time through editing, and only the Qur'an exists in its original form.

The Suhuf Ibrahim

The first holy book is thought to have been given to **Ibrahim**. Known as the Suhuf Ibrahim (scrolls of Ibrahim), it is now **lost**. The Qur'an **mentions** it several times, for example in Qur'an 87:18-19.

The Tawrat

"We sent down the Torah, in which was guidance and light." *Qur'an 5:44*

The Tawrat (Torah) is the book given to **Musa**. It's the main **Jewish** holy book. The Qur'an says it contains the "judgement of Allah" (Qur'an 5:43), so it's **valued** by Muslims. It includes the **Ten Commandments**, basic rules for a **religious life**.

The Zabur

"...to David We gave the book [of Psalms]." *Qur'an 4:163*

The Zabur (Psalms) was given to **Dawud**. It's thought to be linked to the **Psalms** of **David** in the Christian **Bible** and the Jewish **Tenakh**, but many Muslims believe the **original** has been corrupted, perhaps beyond recognition.

The Injil

"We sent ... Our messengers and followed [them] with Jesus ... and gave him the Gospel" *Qur'an 57:27*

Muslims believe Allah gave the Injil to **Isa**. They think the Injil **prophesies** the coming of **Muhammad**. Many Muslims believe the Christian **New Testament** contains the **same ideas** as those given to Isa, but not his exact words. Others think the Injil was **another book** entirely.

Muslims also pay a lot of attention to the guidance and example they get from the following:

HADITH

The **hadith** are **reports** of **Muhammad's** words and actions, recorded by his **followers**. They're **not** in the **Qur'an** — they weren't revealed by **Allah**. **Each one's** been assessed as to how **authentic** it is. There are different **collections** of them, e.g. Sahih al-Bukhari, Sahih Muslim and Sunan Abi Dawud.

SUNNAH

The **sunnah** sets out **Muhammad's way of life**, as recorded in the **hadith**.

- The hadith and the sunnah give valuable advice in addition to the Qur'an, especially on issues concerning daily life — but some Muslims believe it's best just to use the Qur'an, as the hadith might be unreliable.
- Shi'a Muslims also follow the hadith (sayings) of the imams, especially those of Ali.

REVISION TASK

Jibril, Izrail, Tawrat, Zabur, Injil...

...there are lots of names on these pages. Without looking at the book, see if you can write down all the names of the holy books and of the angels, as well as a sentence about each one.

Life after Death

Islam teaches that people will be **judged** on their **behaviour** during their life by **Allah**.

Al-Qadr means predestination

- **Al-Qadr** is the idea that Allah has decided **everything** that will **happen**. This idea appears in teachings such as Sahih al-Bukhari 78:685, in which Muhammad said **vowing** to do something "*does not bring about ... anything [Allah] has not decreed*" — humans **can't** choose to do something Allah hasn't **chosen** for them.

- This might seem to be **contradicted** by the idea of the **Day of Judgement** (see below) when Allah will judge people on the basis of their **actions**. That suggests people have **free will** and can **choose** how they **act** — there'd be **no point** judging them on their actions if what they did had **already** been **decided** by Allah.

- However, many Muslims believe in a **mix** of these two ideas:

<table>
<tr>
<td>SUNNIS</td>
<td>
<ul>
<li>Sunnis tend to believe Allah knows everything that's going to happen — he's above normal laws of time, so knows what humans will choose before they've chosen it.</li>
<li>It's believed humans choose their actions, but Allah has made it impossible that they'll choose anything other than what he's decided.</li>
<li>Some think once someone's chosen to act, the act becomes 'theirs' so they can be judged for it.</li>
</ul>
</td>
<td>SHI'AS</td>
<td>
<ul>
<li>Shi'as focus a bit more on free will.</li>
<li>They often believe Allah has ultimate control and the power to change things in the world if he wants, but that people's lives are usually determined by their choices.</li>
<li>Like Sunnis, they tend to believe Allah knows what's going to happen as he is outside 'human' time — but for Shi'as, what happens is what people choose for themselves.</li>
</ul>
</td>
</tr>
</table>

- To some Muslims, the idea of al-Qadr is **comforting** — if something **bad** has happened, it's **reassuring** to feel it's part of Allah's **plan**. Some people like to feel that they're **guided** to do Allah's **will** by **al-Qadr**.

Yawm ad-Din is the Day of Judgement

- On Yawm ad-Din, Allah **decides** how people will spend the **afterlife**, based on their **behaviour** during their lives. It's then **too late** to **beg forgiveness** for any **wrongdoing**.

- Allah will judge **everyone** — not just Muslims. On Yawm ad-Din, the dead will be **resurrected**. Everyone will receive a **record** of their **good** and **bad** deeds, on which they'll be **judged**.

> **"We will call forth every people with their record [of deeds]."** *Qur'an 17:71*

The idea of judgement is **important** as it encourages Muslims to live their lives in a **good way**. It can be comforting to think **bad** people will be **punished**. Other Muslims think it's best to concentrate on **this life** — they think people should do **good** things anyway, not just because they're focusing on their **afterlife**.

- **Intentions** are also important — **intending** to do something **good** counts, but intending to do something **bad** but **not doing it** doesn't count **against** you (Sahih Muslim 1:233).

Al-Akhirah means the afterlife

Belief in the afterlife — **al-Akhirah** — is a key part of Islam. It's where people go after the Day of Judgement.

The **reward** for good people will be entry into jannah (paradise) — this is a place of peace, happiness and beauty. The Qur'an refers to Paradise as "*Gardens of Pleasure*" (Qur'an 31:8).

> **"...for one whose scales are heavy [with good deeds], He will be in a pleasant life. ...for one whose scales are light, His refuge will be an abyss."** *Qur'an 101:6-9*

For those who have done bad deeds, the punishment is jahannam (hell). The Qur'an describes jahannam as a place of scorching fire and boiling water. Here, those who have ignored Allah's teaching and failed to act righteously will be punished. Allah is merciful though, so they may eventually be sent to paradise.

The Qur'an sometimes mentions a 'barrier' between this world and the next called barzakh, where people's souls stay from the time they die until Yawm ad-Din. Many Muslims focus more on jannah and jahannam than barzakh.

> **"...behind them is a barrier until the Day they are resurrected."** *Qur'an 23:100*

The Day of Judgement — yeah, when is the exam exactly?

Name two concepts linked to the afterlife. [2]

Worship and Duties

There are key actions Muslims try to follow — the **Five Pillars** for **Sunnis**, and **Ten Obligatory Acts** for **Shi'as**.

Sunni Muslims are required to follow the Five Pillars of Islam

SHAHADAH

DECLARATION OF FAITH:
"There is no god but Allah, and Muhammad is his messenger." Muslims should say this **several times** a day. It's said at **birth** and **death**, as well as in the **call to prayer** (adhan) and prayers. People can convert to Islam by saying it. The exact words aren't in the **Qur'an**, but come from passages such as Qur'an 3:18 — *"Allah witnesses that there is no deity except Him"*. It's **essential** to **Shi'a** Muslims too, though it's **not** one of their **Ten Obligatory Acts** (see below). They add *"Ali is the helper of Allah"*, as Ali is **significant** to their faith (see p.24).

SALAH

PRAYER FIVE TIMES A DAY:
The **second most important** duty in Islam. Muslims should pray **five times** a day — at **sunrise**, around **noon**, late **afternoon**, after **sunset**, and late **evening**. See next page for more detail.

ZAKAH

CHARITABLE GIVING:
Each person decides **where** to **donate** their money. Zakah encourages **generosity** and **compassion**. See p.33 for more detail.

SAWM

OBLIGATION TO FAST DURING RAMADAN:
Ramadan is the **ninth month** of the Muslim calendar. Muslims are obliged to fast during it. This teaches **self-discipline**, which brings Muslims **closer** to Allah. See p.33 for more detail.

HAJJ

PILGRIMAGE TO MAKKAH:
Every Muslim should do **hajj** at least once. It's only **obligatory** if you can **afford** it and you're **healthy** enough to do it. See p.34 for more.

Shi'a Muslims follow the Ten Obligatory Acts

Four of these — **salah**, **sawm**, **zakah** and **hajj** — are the same as the **Five Pillars**. There are **six** others:

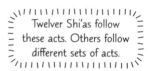
Twelver Shi'as follow these acts. Others follow different sets of acts.

KHUMS — ANNUAL TAX

Khums is a kind of tax Shi'as pay each year on any 'profit' (excess money) they earn, at a rate of 20%. It goes towards supporting Islamic education and anyone descended from Muhammad who's in need.

JIHAD — 'STRUGGLE'

The word means 'struggle' or 'striving'. There are two types of jihad — the 'greater' jihad is Muslims' personal struggle to live a good life, and the 'lesser' jihad is Muslims' struggle to defend Islam against its critics. See p.34 for more.

AMR-BIL-MAROOF AND NAHI ANIL MUNKAR

These come as a pair. The phrase means *"enjoin what is right and forbid what is wrong"* (Qur'an 9:71) — it asks Muslims to encourage good deeds and avoid bad ones.

TAWALLA AND TABARRA

These also come as a pair. They mean 'love' and 'aloofness' — Muslims should love those who follow Allah and they shouldn't associate themselves with anyone who's an 'enemy' of Allah or Muhammad.

Salah is very important

 Salah, the five daily prayers, should ideally take place in a **mosque**, but they can be done anywhere. Sunnis only **combine** the prayers if they have a very **good reason** that **prevents** them praying at five separate times, e.g. if they're **travelling**. Shi'as **combine** some prayers, so they tend to pray **three** times a day rather than **five** — but they still say **all** the **same** prayers.

 Each **prayer cycle** (rak'ah, see p.32) includes saying '**Allahu akbar**' ('**God is great**') multiple times, as well as reciting the **first surah** of the Qur'an (known as the **Fatiha**) and **other verses** from the Qur'an.

> In Muslim countries, the muezzin makes the call to prayer (adhan) from the minaret of a mosque.

Most men are obliged to go to **Friday** prayers (**Jummah**) at the mosque. Requirements **vary**, but a **certain number** of people should be present. The Friday prayers are **led** by an **imam**, who also gives two **sermons**.

Salah keeps Muslims in **close contact** with Allah and encourages moral and spiritual **discipline**. This keeps them from committing **shirk** (see p.26) and increases **taqwa** (reverence for Allah). It's an expression of **solidarity** — doing the same as other Muslims, which is a reminder that everyone's **equal**.

> *"...prayer prohibits immorality and wrongdoing, and the remembrance of Allah is greater."* Qur'an 29:45

There are rituals to follow with Salah

- Wudu (washing before prayer) is important — Muslims must be pure and clean when approaching Allah, both physically and spiritually. Muslims wash their face, arms, feet and part of the hair before prayers. A prayer mat is often used when not praying in a mosque, in order to ensure cleanliness.

- Muslims should face Makkah in Saudi Arabia when praying. The direction of Makkah is called the qiblah.

- The rak'ah is a set prayer ritual. It may be repeated several times at each prayer session. Each rak'ah involves standing, then kneeling, then putting your forehead to the ground as a sign of submission to Allah. If several Muslims are praying in one place, then the rak'ah is done together at the same time.

Shi'a prayers are a bit different. Shi'as touch their foreheads to a clay or wooden tablet during the rak'ah — they believe putting their forehead on something natural is what Muhammad advised. The tablet is often made of clay from Karbala, where Husayn was killed (p.35), to remind Shi'as of his sacrifice.

 When at the mosque, women and men pray separately — so people concentrate on Allah rather than on the opposite sex.

 This has changed in some mosques though, where mixed prayer is allowed.

- Many Muslims perform salah in the home rather than at the mosque, particularly women. It's seen as an important way for children to learn about Islam. Some Muslim families may have a room just for salah.

Worship and Duties

Zakah is charitable giving

- Zakah involves **redistributing** wealth. Muslims think wealth's **given** by Allah, so should be used to **serve** him.
- The amount is usually **2.5%** of a person's wealth each year. Muslims can decide how much to give and who they want to donate it to. It's often used to help Muslims who are **less well off**, or given to **charities** or **mosques**.
- It's a sign of **concern** for others and encourages **generosity**.

  Some **Shi'as** pay **khums** (see p.31) in **addition** to zakah.

> *"Zakah...[is] for bringing hearts together."* Qur'an 9:60

This verse also lists who zakah is for, including the *"poor and... needy"*.

Sawm is fasting during Ramadan

- Muslims must fast between **sunrise** and **sunset** during the month of **Ramadan**. The Muslim calendar is **lunar** (determined by the **moon**), so Ramadan isn't always at the **same time** of the **solar** (sun) year.
- Muslims eat just before sunrise (**suhur**) and just after sunset (**iftar**). The fast is often broken **slowly** with **dates**, before a bigger meal later. **Iftar** is often eaten with **family** or **friends**, or sometimes at the **mosque**.

> *"O you who have believed, decreed upon you is fasting ... that you may become righteous..."* Qur'an 2:183

There are exceptions to the obligation to fast:

- **Children** don't have to fast until they're about **12 years old**. **Old people** (there's no **specific** age) **don't** have to fast either.
- People can be excused for **medical** reasons. Women who are **pregnant**, **breastfeeding** or **menstruating** can also be excused. It's fine to take **medicine** which has to be **regular**, e.g. antibiotics. If you're on a **journey**, you can be excused too.
- If you've **missed** a few days of the fast, Qur'an 2:184 says that you should **make up for it**, either by **fasting** for the **same number** of days later on, or by giving **food** to someone who might **need** it.

- **Sawm** doesn't just involve **not eating** or **drinking**, but also **abstaining** from **other things** such as **sex**, **smoking** and listening to **music**. Muslims should also try hard to avoid **bad thoughts** or **actions**.
- **Ramadan** is a time of both **physical** and **moral self-discipline**, and a time of **obedience** to Allah. It's supposed to help Muslims understand **hunger**, and so makes them more **willing** to help others.
- It's also a time to show **publicly** that **Allah** matters more than any **physical needs**.

Laylat al-Qadr falls during Ramadan

- **Laylat al-Qadr** is the **Night of Destiny** or **Power**.
- Muslims believe Muhammad received at least part of the Qur'an during this night. So Ramadan is also a time of **thanksgiving** for the Qur'an — during Ramadan it's read from **beginning** to **end** at the **mosque**.
- Laylat al-Qadr is the **holiest night** of the year — the Qur'an says it's *"better than a thousand months"* (Qur'an 97:3) and many Muslims spend the **whole** night at the mosque to **celebrate** it, praying and listening to readings of the Qur'an.
- It's **important** because many Muslims believe Allah will **forgive** their **sins** on this night.

| **Worship and Duties**

The **hajj** is an important action for a Muslim to do. Around **2 million** Muslims go each year.

The Hajj is the pilgrimage to Makkah

"...proclaim to the people the Hajj..." *Qur'an 22:27*

- Muslims must make the pilgrimage at least **once** in their lifetime, as long as they can **afford** it and they're **healthy** enough to cope with the journey.
- It has to happen in the Muslim month of Dhu'l-Hijja to **count**.
- **Adam**, **Ibrahim** and **Isma'il** are all associated with **Makkah** and **Muhammad** lived there, so it's a holy place.
- **All pilgrims** wear simple white clothing (**ihram**) so they're **equal** before Allah.

1 The Ka'aba is in Makkah — it's a giant **stone cube** covered with **black cloth**. Some Muslims think **Ibrahim** and **Isma'il** built it as a place of worship — Qur'an 2:127 suggests they did. Others think **Adam** built it. It's the **holiest place** in Islam. Muslims must do **seven circuits** anticlockwise of the Ka'aba, touching the stone if possible — this ritual is called the **tawaf**.

2 Next, a pilgrim must make **seven journeys** between the hills of **Safa** and **Marwa** (where Hajar, Ibrahim's wife and servant, searched for water for their son Isma'il). This part of the pilgrimage is called the **sa'y**.

3 Pilgrims then draw **water** from the **Zamzam Well**, which **Allah** made for Hajar.

4 Then pilgrims go to **Mount Arafat** to **stand** and pray for Allah's **forgiveness**. This is where Muslims believe **Adam** was **forgiven** after being **thrown out** of Eden and also where the **Day of Judgement** will take place.

5 The pilgrims spend the night at **Muzdalifa**, a valley between **Arafat** and **Mina**, where they collect **pebbles**.

6 The pebbles are then thrown at three **pillars** in **Mina**, to symbolise driving the **devil** away — **Ibrahim** is believed to have once thrown stones at **Shaytan** (the devil). This happens on **Id ul-Adha** (see p.35).

The title '**hajji**' is given to those who **complete** the hajj. Many find the **hajj** helps their **faith** and increases **unity** between Muslims. Some **hadith** say it cleanses the hajji of **all sins**.

"he will return (after Hajj free from all sins) as if he were born anew" *Sahih al-Bukhari 26:596*

There are two kinds of Jihad

Jihad means 'striving' or 'struggle' and is often **misunderstood** by non-Muslims. It's one of the **Ten Obligatory Acts** for **Shi'as** (see p.31) but it's part of **Sunni** Islam too. Most Muslims believe there are **two kinds**:

The Greater Jihad

- This is every Muslim's struggle to **obey** Allah, **follow** his teachings and become a **better** Muslim.
- It's the **greater struggle** because it's **individual** and **personal**. Qur'an 35:18 says *"no bearer of burdens will bear the burden of another"* (burdens mean sins), so you and you alone will be held **responsible** for your **behaviour**. If you're not a good Muslim, it's **harder** to help make the world better (**lesser jihad**).

The Lesser Jihad

- This is the **struggle** to make the world a **better place**. Part of this means struggling against wrongs such as **poverty** and **injustice**.
- Part of it is the struggle to **defend Islam** against threats. It can be in **peaceful** ways, such as helping others be good Muslims.
- The Qur'an and Islamic law say that actual fighting should only be in **self-defence** and **not** against people who **aren't fighting** (**non-combatants**). Qur'an 4:75 says Muslims should fight on behalf of people being **oppressed**.
- **Islamic terrorists** claim the Qur'an supports **violence** to **defend** Islam against **oppression**. The vast **majority** of Muslims **condemn** this and think that Islamic terrorists aren't **true** Muslims.

When Islam began, Muslims fought to survive as people of other religions persecuted them. The Qur'an reflects this struggle, which is why it refers to defending Islam against its enemies.

"Permission [to fight] has been given to those who are being fought." *Qur'an 22:39*

"...if they cease, then there is to be no aggression except against the oppressors" *Qur'an 2:193*

And that's the last of the duties...

You might see some of the Arabic words spelt slightly differently, e.g. zakat rather than zakah or Eid al-Adha rather than Id ul-Adha. Make sure you always stick to one spelling in the exam.

Festivals Islam

There are several festivals throughout the year. Id ul-Adha and Id ul-Fitr are important to Sunnis and Shi'as.

Id ul-Adha *focuses on the importance of obeying Allah*

- Id ul-Adha is a festival celebrating complete obedience to Allah, as it commemorates the time when Ibrahim nearly sacrificed his own son, Isma'il. It's a very important festival and it forms part of the hajj.

- Muslims should attend mosque on Id ul-Adha — the service includes communal prayers and a sermon focused on the importance of obedience to Allah and the lessons to be learnt from Ibrahim and Isma'il.

- An animal is often sacrificed and divided up into three — a third is kept by the family, a third goes to relatives or neighbours and a third goes to the poor.

> Ibrahim dreamt that Allah told him to sacrifice Isma'il. He told Isma'il about it and Isma'il agreed it had to be done. But at the last minute, Allah told Ibrahim to sacrifice a ram in place of Isma'il, so Isma'il survived. It was a test of Ibrahim's loyalty to Allah.
>
> > " '...my son, indeed I have seen in a dream that I [must] sacrifice you ...' He said, 'O my father, do as you are commanded.' "
> > *Qur'an 37:102*

- Id ul-Adha is a time of communal joy and festivity lasting up to four days. Muslims dress up in their best clothes and spend time with family and friends. Presents are often exchanged.

Id ul-Fitr *marks the end of Ramadan*

- Id ul-Fitr is at the end of Ramadan (see p.33). It's a day of thanksgiving to Allah for giving Muslims the strength to fast for a month.

- It's a joyful festival which also celebrates the fact that Muslims have completed the fourth pillar of Islam by observing sawm, and therefore have become closer to Allah.

DONATIONS	THE FESTIVAL
Muslims pay a special zakah for Id ul-Fitr. Usually around £5, it helps Muslims who are less well off celebrate Id ul-Fitr as well. It's often given out in the form of food by charities or mosques.	The festival involves a service with prayers and a sermon (at the mosque or outside), and a meal to break the fast. Like Id ul-Adha, it's a time of celebration, when family and friends meet up, presents are exchanged and people wear their best clothes.

> Thousands of people attend celebrations of both Ids in the UK — many Muslims find it important for community cohesion between Muslims and people of other faiths.

Ashura *commemorates the death of Husayn*

- Id ul-Adha and Id ul-Fitr are important for both Sunnis and Shi'as, but Ashura is mostly a Shi'a festival.

Originally, Ashura was a compulsory day of fasting for all Muslims.	⇨	When Muhammad said Muslims should observe sawm during Ramadan, fasting on Ashura became voluntary.	⇨	Sunnis now tend to think of it as a day of atonement. Many Sunnis fast, but it's not compulsory. It's believed that fasting may absolve people of their minor sins in the previous year.

- Ashura is important for Shi'as because it was the day Husayn, Ali's son and Muhammad's grandson (see p.24), was killed in a battle. The ten days up to and including Ashura (Ashura is the tenth day) are a period of mourning for Shi'as. Mosques often provide free meals for people during the ten day period.

- On Ashura, Shi'as wear black as a sign of mourning. There are often public processions (there's usually one in London) and 'passion plays', in which the story of Husayn is performed. Poems or stories about Husayn are often read out.

- Some Shi'as hurt themselves to commemorate Husayn's suffering. This is banned in some countries.

- For Shi'as, Ashura is a reminder of the suffering the Shi'a community has experienced — Shi'as have been persecuted as a minority. The processions are sometimes used as protests against injustice.

Feeling festive...?

Why not celebrate with a good old exam-style question?

Explain two ways in which Id ul-Fitr is celebrated. Include examples from Muslim teaching. [5]

Beliefs, Teachings and Practices — Islam

Revision Summary

There was a lot in that section, so now it's your chance to find out how much you **remember**. These are **exam-style questions**, so you can get an idea of how **long** and **detailed** your answers have to be. If you're **stuck** on anything, **go back** to the relevant page in the section and then **try** the question **again**.

We'll start off with some straightforward 1 mark multiple choice questions.

1) Which of the following is the belief in angels?
   a) Tawhid   b) Imamah   c) Malaikah   d) Nubuwwah

2) Which of the following is the concept of messengership?
   a) Nubuwwah   b) Risalah   c) Hadith   d) Prophets

3) Which of the following describes the way of life set out by Muhammad?
   a) Qur'an   b) Hadith   c) Salah   d) Sunnah

4) Which of the following is the obligation to fast during Ramadan?
   a) Sawm   b) Salah   c) Shahadah   d) Zakah

These questions are worth 2 marks. You need to make two brief points in your answer.

5) Give two of the Usul ad-Din.

6) Name two of the prophets, other than Muhammad.

7) Give two of the Ten Obligatory Acts.

8) Give two exceptions to the obligation to fast during Ramadan.

These are 4 mark questions. To get full marks, you need to develop the points you make.

9) Explain two ways in which belief in Muhammad might influence Muslims today.

10) Explain two ways in which beliefs in angels might influence Muslims today.

11) Explain two contrasting ways of giving to charity in Islam.

12) Explain two contrasting understandings of Ashura.

These questions are worth 5 marks, so you need to develop and explain your answer. You also need to include Muslim teachings in your answer.

13) Explain two Muslim ideas about the Qur'an.

14) Explain two Muslim teachings about judgement.

15) Explain two reasons why Laylat al-Qadr is important for Muslims.

16) Explain two reasons why performing hajj is important for Muslims.

> Your points need to be nice and clear in the longer answer questions. This means you need to make sure your writing is well organised.

And the big one — this is a 12 mark question. Use the bullet point list below to help you plan your answer — the list gives you the things you need to include. Try coming up with arguments for and against the statement before you start, so you don't leave anything out.

17) 'The most important thing a Muslim can do is pray five times a day.'
    Evaluate this statement. Your answer should include the following:

- examples from Islamic teachings
- arguments that support the statement
- arguments that disagree with the statement
- a conclusion

> There's advice on writing essays in the 'Do Well in Your Exam' section.

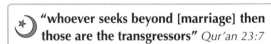

Sexuality and Sexual Relationships

Christianity & Islam

You must be aware of **religious** and **non-religious** views in Britain, and be able to give **two** or more contrasting religious views on **homosexuality** and **sex before marriage**, with at least one being **Christian**.

Christianity *and* Islam *have* similar attitudes *to sex*

Traditionally, both religions teach that the only correct context for sexual activity is within marriage — sex outside of it is seen as a **sin**. This means **cohabitation** (living together unmarried) isn't approved of.

✝ **"Sexuality is ordered to the conjugal love of man and woman"** *Catechism of the Catholic Church (2360)*

☾ **"whoever seeks beyond [marriage] then those are the transgressors"** *Qur'an 23:7*

conjugal *within marriage*

The Catechism also says that sex is *"unitive"* and *"procreative"* — to bring married couples together as one and for having children.

- Christians and Muslims are urged to keep sex within marriage for positive reasons as well — marriage is believed to make sex **more special**. Both religions stress the importance of **enjoying** sex — the Song of Solomon in the Bible contains poems celebrating sexual desire and relationships.
- 'Strict' members of both faiths think the principle of only having sex within marriage still applies. More **liberal** members might see this as outdated, although they still tend to see marriage as the **ideal**.
- **Promiscuity** (having multiple sexual partners) is often seen as wrong in both religions.

Sex outside of marriage is considered normal in British society

- Many British people think promiscuity is acceptable, especially now **contraception** (see p.38) is widely available — though a **large** number of sexual partners is seen more **negatively**.
- **Humanists** accept sex outside of marriage as long as it causes **no harm** to anyone. **Atheists** tend to accept it too.

Homosexuality *is a disputed topic*

The Christian and Muslim scriptures seem to say that homosexual sex is **wrong**.

The story of **Sodom** (Genesis 19:3-25) is used by **Christianity and Islam** to argue against homosexuality.
- The city's destroyed after the men in Sodom demand sex with two male angels God sent, which some people use to show that homosexuality is wrong.
- However, the angels say God sent them to destroy the city because of sin... so some people argue that God was going to destroy it anyway — not because the men wanted sex with the angels.

✝ **"Under no circumstances can [homosexual acts] be approved"** *Catechism of the Catholic Church (2357)*

☾ **"you approach men with desire, instead of women ... you are a transgressing people"** *Qur'an 7:81*

- The texts don't condemn people who have homosexual feelings but don't act upon them. This means some people who are homosexual and religious opt for **celibacy** (they don't have sexual relationships).
- They only condemn sex between men, not between **women**, which is hardly mentioned. (Though it's often **frowned upon** because male homosexuality is.)

> The first same-sex marriages in the UK took place in 2014 — see p.40 for Christian and Muslim views.

Homosexuality is considered normal in British society

Even many religious people argue that as the scriptures were written in a different **cultural context** from ours, we can't apply their standards today. Generally, the religions **condemn homophobia** and they're becoming more accepting of homosexuality.

EXAM TIP

Both religions have quite similar views on these topics...

...but remember there are different views within each religion. You often have to give two views in the exam and you get marks for the level of detail, so learn them well.

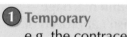

| Christianity & Islam | **Contraception** |

You need to learn about the contrasting religious views on contraception.

Contraception prevents a woman becoming pregnant

Contraception is also known as birth control and is used to **stop** a woman **conceiving**. There are **two types**:

1 Temporary
e.g. the contraceptive pill or condoms

2 Permanent (also called sterilisation)
e.g. a vasectomy

Using contraception is sometimes called 'family planning'.

Most **atheists** and **humanists** have no objection to contraception:

> They think it's better if people only have children if they really **want** them.

> Contraception allows people to **choose** when to have sex, by limiting the risk of pregnancy.

> Some types also reduce the risk of **STIs** (sexually transmitted infections).

Both religions have a range of views about contraception

The table below **summarises** the main Christian and Muslim arguments **for** and **against** contraception:

	Views IN FAVOUR of contraception	Views AGAINST contraception
CHRISTIANITY	• Some Roman Catholics are highly in favour of contraception because of concerns about **STIs**. • The Anglican, Methodist and Presbyterian Churches are in favour of contraception, suggesting that it lets parents **plan** their family in a **responsible** way. • Many Christians believe that contraception should be a question of **individual conscience**. They see it as positive that women can **control** when they get pregnant.	• The Catechism of the Catholic Church 2367 says that married couples should *"transmit human life"* (i.e. have children). • Humanae Vitae 14 says that anything *"deliberately contraceptive"* is *"intrinsically wrong"*. • The Church says contraception may lead to **promiscuity** (p.37) • Some Christians object to forms of contraception that might destroy a fertilised egg, such as the morning after pill — this is because they see it as being the same as **abortion** (see p.51).
	• The Catholic Church does allow **natural** contraception — only having sex at the **less fertile** times in a woman's menstrual cycle. • Christians are divided over sterilisation, which prevents people ever having children.	
ISLAM	• The hadith Sahih al-Bukhari 62:136 is believed to **support** the use of contraception. • Contraception is sometimes considered acceptable if having another child may cause **harm** to the **mother**, any **existing children** or to the **potential child**, e.g. if the family can't afford to feed another child.	• Another hadith, Sahih al-Bukhari 34:432, says **conception** is **Allah's will** and suggests people shouldn't try to avoid it. • As with some Christians, some Muslims **also** view forms of contraception that might destroy a fertilised egg as the same as **abortion**.
	• Muslims believe it's the right of both husband and wife to try for children, so both partners must **agree** to contraception. • Only 'reversible' methods are allowed — sterilisation and vasectomies are usually not accepted.	

EXAM QUESTION

Remember that religious views focus on marital sex...

Have a go at this exam-style question using the information you've learnt on this page.
Explain two contrasting religious beliefs about contraception.

[4]

Marriage and Divorce

The **views** of many Christians and Muslims on marriage and divorce have **changed less** than those of **wider British society** over the past few decades.

Marriage in the UK — things have changed

Non-religious attitudes to **marriage**, **divorce** and **cohabitation** are very different now to what they were in the past.

Marriage
- The number of marriages taking place in the UK each year has been **decreasing** over the last **40 years**.
- Although many **non-religious** people still see marriage as **important**, others see it as **unnecessary**.
- People are also tending to get married **later** in life, and many people have **children** without being married.
- **Same-sex** marriages are now **legal** across the UK. Many people see this as a good thing because it creates **equality**.

Cohabitation
- It's now more **common** (and **acceptable**) for people to cohabit (**live together**) — either **before** marrying or **instead of** getting married.
- Cohabiting couples don't have the same **legal rights** as married ones though.

Divorce
- Divorce has become far more **common**. Non-religious people often see it as **sensible** if the couple don't get on, as they'll be **happier** if they divorce.
- Some argue parents fighting can **harm** children more than divorce.
- However, many **religious** people try to **avoid** divorce if at all possible.

Christians and Muslims both think marriage is very important

- For Christians, marriage reflects the **union** of **Jesus** with his **followers**.
- Muslims believe that marriage is **Allah's will**. According to a **hadith**, Muhammad said that marriage was **half** of a Muslim's **faith**.

>  **"marry the unmarried among you"** *Qur'an 24:32*

> **"He created for you ... mates that you may find tranquillity in them; and he placed between you affection..."** *Qur'an 30:21*

Christian and Muslim views are mostly similar

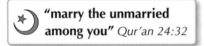

Purpose of marriage

✝ In Christianity, marriage is a **covenant** (contract) between **two** people to offer **love**, **support** and **commitment**, and to have **children**.

☪ Islam is **family-oriented**, so marriage is strongly recommended. It provides **companionship**, **love** and **stability**, and is a secure environment for **having children** (**procreation**).

Polygamy

✝ **Nearly all Christians** see polygamy (marriage to **multiple** people) as **wrong**.

👍 Some Muslims believe the Qur'an allows polygamy. A man should only take multiple wives if he can treat them equally.

👎 Polygamy is criticised by many Muslims, in particular the fact it's only allowed for men. Polygamy is **illegal** in the UK, but polygamous marriages are **accepted** if they took place **elsewhere**.

Adultery

✝ **Faithfulness** in marriage is important — adultery is forbidden in the **Ten Commandments** (Exodus 20:14).

☪ Adultery is a **sin** — the Qur'an calls it **"evil"** (Qur'an 17:32). Some Muslim countries punish it severely.

Theme A — Relationships and Families

Islam & Christianity	# Marriage and Divorce

Islamic marriage is called nikah

- **Nikah** is the name for marriage under **shari'ah**.
- To have their marriage recognised as legal in Britain, Muslim couples must also have a civil wedding ceremony.
- Qur'an 4:1-24 clearly sets out **rules** for **who** people can marry and how much different people **inherit**.
- Some Muslims have **arranged marriages**. This is where the parents will choose a marriage partner for their child. However, both potential partners have the **right to say no** to marrying their parents' choice.

> shari'ah
> *Islamic law*

Same-sex marriage is controversial in Christianity and Islam

	👍 **Views and actions IN FAVOUR of same-sex marriage**	👎 **Views and actions AGAINST same-sex Marriage**
CHRISTIANITY	• Some Church of England clergy hold **blessings** for same-sex couples after they marry in **civil** (non-religious) ceremonies. • Anglican supporters of same-sex marriage say Christians should be **loving** to **all** and should support anyone who wants to marry. • Members of the congregation (particularly **younger people**) within the Catholic Church and the Church of England tend to be more likely to be in favour of same-sex marriage than their church leaders.	• The decision to legalise same-sex marriage in the UK was **criticised** by the **Catholic Church** and the **Church of England**. Many members of the clergy are against it. *The Catholic Church is more strongly against homosexual relationships and same-sex marriage than most other Christians.* "The Church of England affirms, according to our Lord's teaching, that marriage is ... a union... of one man with one woman." *Canon B30* • Those in the Anglican church who are against same-sex marriage say it's a **sin**.
		Many Christians and Muslims believe it's wrong because one **purpose** of marriage is having **children**.
ISLAM	• Some Muslims argue that homosexuality is **normal** and that it's good for same-sex couples to have the **chance to be married**, as marriage is important in Islam. • Since Muslims are a **minority** in Britain, they should **help out** another minority by supporting same-sex marriage, regardless of their individual views on homosexuality.	• Many Muslims believe **homosexual sex** is **forbidden** by the Qur'an (see p.37). • The **Muslim Council of Britain** argued that the law legalising same-sex marriage in the UK was **unnecessary** because **civil partnerships** gave same-sex couples **equal rights** anyway and that same-sex marriage **undermined** the definition of marriage as between a man and a woman.

Religious views on cohabitation vary

👎 Some Christians, including the Catholic Church, tend to be **against** cohabitation — they disagree with sex outside marriage. ✝

👍 Many Christians accept cohabitation, especially as **preparation** for **marriage**. **Pope Francis** has recognised it can be hard for people to marry, e.g. for financial reasons — but they should be **encouraged** to **marry** eventually.

☪ In Islam cohabitation often **isn't accepted** as it tends to involve sex outside of marriage.

In a book called 'Not Just Good, but Beautiful', Pope Francis said marriage is 'indispensable' to society.

Theme A — Relationships and Families

Marriage and Divorce

Different Christian Churches have varying attitudes to divorce

There are different views as to whether divorce is permissible, or even possible.

 Impossible The Roman Catholic Church says it's impossible to divorce (Catechism of the Catholic Church 2382). Marriage is a sacrament — God made the couple one flesh, which can't be undone. However, a marriage can be annulled (declared void) if the couple never had sex or if a partner didn't consent to or understand the marriage, or refused to have children.

 Possible
- The Church of England says divorce is possible and accepts that some marriages fail. Divorcees can usually re-marry in church.
- Nonconformist Churches (e.g. Baptists and Methodists) will usually re-marry divorcees.

Some members of these Churches disagree with this, and individual ministers may not be willing to re-marry divorcees if it goes against their conscience.

- Jesus himself was generally anti-divorce. In Matthew 19:8-9 NIV, he says divorce and remarriage are only allowed if someone's partner's been unfaithful.

> "A man [and] his wife ... will become one flesh. ... what God has joined together, let no one separate." *Mark 10:7-9 NIV*

- Some Christians view an unhappy marriage as a waste of two lives, and so see divorce as preferable.

In Islam divorce is the last resort, but it's accepted

- Divorce is permitted, but only as a last resort.

> "Of all the lawful acts the most detestable to Allah is divorce." *Sunan Abi Dawud 12:2173*

- If things aren't going well, an arbiter from each family should be appointed to try to sort things out. Muslims see reconciliation as particularly important when the couple have children.
- If the marriage cannot be saved, Qur'an 2:226-241 lays out the conditions under which divorce can happen. They are different for men and women.

A man can divorce his wife 'by talaq'

To divorce 'by talaq', a man has to say 'I divorce you' to his wife three times. However, it's often recommended that it should be said once on three separate occasions and that there's a three-month waiting period, to allow time for reflection. The waiting period also ensures the woman is not pregnant.

There are three ways a woman can divorce her husband

Depending on the circumstances, a woman can divorce her husband in one of three ways:

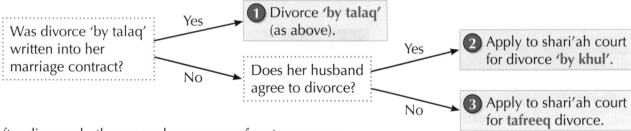

- After divorce, both men and women are free to re-marry.
- As Islamic law isn't part of British law, these kinds of divorce dissolve the nikah (p.40), but don't count as a legal divorce if the couple also had a civil marriage — they would have to get a civil divorce too.

Phew, what a lot of different opinions...

In the exam, you might be asked to give similar or contrasting beliefs about marriage and divorce — try comparing Muslim and Christian views so you understand the differences and similarities.

Christianity & Islam	# Families

As the saying goes, 'you can choose your GCSEs, but you can't choose your family'. Or something like that...

Family is important to Christians and Muslims

- Ideally, a **stable** family can give a child a sense of **identity** and a feeling of **security**. They'll learn how to **behave**, how to give and receive **love**, and about **right** and **wrong**.
- Many Christians and Muslims think it's best for a child to have a **father** and a **mother** present (ideally the child's **biological** parents), so that they grow up with one **role model** of each sex. Ideally, the couple would be **married**, as it's believed this provides more **stability**.
- For **religious** people, family life can be a way of introducing their **children** to their **faith**. The table shows some of the ways Christians and Muslims **link** family life and faith:

	CHRISTIANITY	ISLAM
Purpose of family life	Family life is important for most Christians. It's seen as a way to build a stable society. "family is 'the first and vital cell of society'." *Pope John Paul II, Familiaris Consortio 42 (Catholic teachings on family)* Festivals such as Christmas and Easter have a strong emphasis on celebration within the family.	Many Muslims think family life teaches people to be kind, considerate and affectionate. Strong family ties help strengthen the Muslim community — the ummah.
Educating children in the faith at home	Many Christians believe it's important to have children and educate them in the faith — see for example Catechism of the Catholic Church 2226 and this quote: "bring [your children] up in the training and instruction of the Lord." *Ephesians 6:4 NIV* This might include activities at home such as reading the child Bible stories, or teaching them about prayer by saying grace (giving thanks) before meals.	Following Muslim food laws by having halal food in the home helps introduce the child to Islam.
Educating children in the faith outside the home	Many churches offer help in raising children, through Sunday schools. These schools aim to teach Christian morals and ideals through the study of Bible stories.	Mosques often have schools (madrasahs) to teach children about Islam. They learn Arabic so they can read the Qur'an and say prayers. They're also taught from the hadith and sunnah (see p.29).
Ceremonies to introduce children to the faith	Children become part of the faith at baptism, and this develops as they attend church and prepare for confirmation (see p.14).	Rituals such as aqiqah (a naming ritual) and the bismillah ceremony, which marks the start of the child's religious education, help connect the child to the faith.
Treatment of parents	Children are asked to honour their parents — to look after and respect them (Exodus 20:12).	The Qur'an asks people to care for their parents — Muslims place importance on the extended family too. "We have enjoined upon man, to his parents, good treatment." *Qur'an 46:15*

Families

Family life in the UK has changed

For a long time, the **nuclear family** was seen in Britain as the ideal family model.
Religious families are **more likely** than the UK average to follow this model.

1.8 children is the average...

Today, it's common to find:

- **single-parent** families
- **unmarried** couples
- **reconstituted** (or **blended**) families
- **extended** families living together
- **same-sex** parents

nuclear family
A married man and woman, and their children

reconstituted (or **blended**) family
A couple and their children from previous relationships.

extended family
A family which includes grandparents, cousins etc.

Some people worry it's bad for children to grow up with same-sex parents, because they will only have **role models** from **one sex**.

Others argue that same-sex couples can provide a **stable**, **loving** home, which is what's important.

Extended families living together has become **more common** as people **live longer**, house prices **rise** and both parents **work**.

- Parents and children might **share** a home with grandparents to **save** money on housing.
- The grandparents can be **looked after** by the parents but also **help** look after the children.

Christians try to welcome different families

Welcoming

- Whatever their opinions on divorce and homosexuality, many Christians focus on making sure reconstituted families and single or same-sex parents feel **welcome** in church.
- It is **important** that families remain **connected** to the church, particularly so that any **children** will still be brought up in a **Christian way**.

> "[Catholics should take] solicitous care to make sure that [divorcees] do not consider themselves as separated from the Church." *Pope John Paul II, Familiaris Consortio 84*

Less welcoming

- Some Christians' views on divorce and homosexuality make it **difficult** for them to **accept** certain types of family.
- The Catholic Church is more strongly **against** same-sex parenting than many other denominations. Catholics believe homosexuality is **wrong** and God created men and women to form a family.
- Divorced Catholics aren't allowed to take **communion** (see p.12), which could mean they feel **unwelcome** in church.

Muslim views are changing

Some Muslims are **accepting** of **divorced people** and **reconstituted families**, while others are **less so**.

Many Muslims would frown upon **same-sex parents** because they see homosexuality as wrong.
Some Muslims believe that, whatever their **personal opinion**, they should be **accepting** of same-sex parents because no one is **without sin**, so they shouldn't **judge**.
Others are in favour of **same-sex** parents.

The **extended family** is also **important** in Islam, particularly for offering love and support.

EXAM QUESTION

It's never simple, is it...

Have a quick go at this exam question, just for a fun break...
Give two religious attitudes towards divorcees.

[2]

Gender Equality

Discrimination based on gender is widespread

Gender discrimination is a problem in British society, although the situation's gradually improving.

- **Gender stereotypes** (e.g. **women** being more **emotional** and **men** being more **confident**, or **fixed roles** for men and women) are now seen by many people as **false, unnecessary** and **damaging** to both genders.
- Some people argue there is still a **long way to go** before women are treated equally to men, e.g. as **well below half** of MPs are women. Others think the genders are now treated more or less **equally**. There have been **shifts** in gender balance in some areas, e.g. women are now more likely than men to go to university.

Men and women often have different roles in the home

Having different roles doesn't necessarily mean either are **unequal**,
but these **fixed ideas** make it **hard** for **either** gender to do the **opposite role**.

WOMEN
- **Taking care** of the **family** and **home** is often seen as the woman's role.
- Entitled to **52 weeks' maternity leave**, with **39 weeks** paid.
  - This is more than men, to reflect the fact that women **give birth** and many women **breastfeed**.
- Women often encounter **problems** in the **workplace** after taking time off to have children — many find their male colleagues have been **promoted** in the meantime, or struggle to afford **childcare** which would allow them to return to work.
- Women often still do **more housework** than men, even if they're working.

MEN
- The man's role has traditionally been to **earn money** to **support** the family.
  - This means that many men **don't** get to **look after** and **spend time** with their **children**.
- If the parents don't choose to take shared parental leave, men are only entitled to **2 weeks'** paid **paternity leave**. Some feel 2 weeks is **too little**.

> **Shared parental leave (SPL)**, introduced in the UK in **2015**, gives parents the option to **share** the time off work to look after their child in its first year. SPL involves the mother **giving up** part of her maternity leave so that the father can spend that time with the child instead. **Very few** fathers have taken SPL so far.

There are problems with equality in the workplace

Contrary to what many people believe, women have **always worked**.

In the past...	• Women were prevented from doing many jobs, by law or by other people. • Some had to stop work when they married. • Women were often paid less than men for the same job, or offered jobs with less responsibility and lower pay.

These **three** pieces of **legislation** have helped to **reduce** gender inequalities in the workplace:

1 Equal Pay Act 1970

2 Sex Discrimination Act 1975

These made gender discrimination **illegal**, e.g. by saying **both genders** had to be **paid** the **same amount** and have the **same working conditions** for the **same job**.

3 Equality Act 2010
This brought all the legislation together in **one act**.
It also made **positive action** legal.
The Act allows for '**occupational requirements**'.

positive action
action to help a group that's underrepresented in a profession or organisation. E.g. if a male-dominated company has two equally-qualified candidates for a job, it's legal for them to pick the female candidate to help women become better represented in the company.

occupational requirements
objective reasons why a certain group is best for a job. This means it's legal to e.g. only offer a male role in a play to male actors.

Despite these laws, some **problems remain**.

Today...	• There are professions in which one gender is underrepresented. Nursing or midwifery are seen as women's jobs, while building or firefighting are seen as men's. • Women are underrepresented in positions of authority, e.g. as politicians or company directors. • Many women still face discrimination at work, such as receiving lower pay, not being considered for promotion or being sexually harassed, although it's illegal.

It can be hard to prove discrimination happened. E.g. it's hard to tell if you're being paid less than someone else in the same job.

Gender Equality

Traditional gender roles were, and often still are, **supported** by **Christianity** and **Islam**.

The Bible is a bit unclear on the status of women

- The Bible gives messages both against and in favour of gender discrimination.

> "There is neither ... male [nor] female, for you are all one in Christ Jesus." *Galatians 3:28 NIV*

> "I do not permit a woman to teach or to assume authority over a man; she must be quiet." *1 Timothy 2:12 NIV*

- The Bible also says that wives should do as their husbands **tell them**:

> "Wives, submit ... to your own husbands as you do to the Lord. For the husband is the head of the wife as Christ is the head of the church..." *Ephesians 5:22-23 NIV*

- Many Christians say this reflects the ideas of society at the time, and doesn't correspond with Jesus's attitude towards women.
- Some of Jesus's followers were women, e.g. Mary and Martha (Luke 10:38-42), and he treated them equally.

Different denominations have different approaches to gender equality

Many Christians now believe men and women should be **equal**.

- The Catechism of the Catholic Church 1938 mentions *"sinful inequalities"* and says Catholics **fight against this**.
  - Despite this, the Catholic Church is still **more focused** on **traditional** gender roles than other denominations.

> "society should create and develop conditions favouring work in the home [for women]" *Pope John Paul II, Familiaris Consortio 23*

- For most of Christian history, women weren't allowed to be **priests**. This is no longer the case — women can now be **ministers** in most **Protestant** denominations, and **Anglican priests** and **bishops**. But they can't be **Roman Catholic** or **Orthodox** priests.

In Islam, men and women are equal but have different roles

- Men and women have an equal obligation to Allah in terms of prayer, fasting, pilgrimage and charity.

> "Indeed, the Muslim men and Muslim women, the believing men and believing women, the obedient men and obedient women ... the charitable men and charitable women, the fasting men and fasting women... and the men who remember Allah often and the women who do so — for them Allah has prepared forgiveness and a great reward." *Qur'an 33:35*

- Some teachings might suggest men are superior. But they're usually taken to mean that men and women just have different roles within the community — men are responsible for providing for the family, and women are responsible for the home.

> "Men are in charge of women by [right of] what Allah has given one over the other and what they spend [for maintenance] from their wealth" *Qur'an 4:34*

- There's a range of views among Muslims on women in the workplace:

> It's OK for women to work.

> Women should only work if essential or to fill jobs more suited to women, e.g. midwifery.

> Work is a distraction from women's primary role of looking after the family and home.

For many Muslim women wearing **modest clothing**, often including a **head covering**, is an important part of Islam. However, some people believe Muslim women are **forced** to wear this clothing, and see it as a way of **oppressing** women. Muslim women argue it's their **choice**, and that any **ban** on head coverings would be just as oppressive, as it **takes away** that choice.

Hmmm... it's a tricky issue.

Learn specific examples to give in your answer, such as jobs where one gender is underrepresented.

Revision Summary

You might think you're done with this section... but I'm afraid there are a few **questions** for you to do first, just to see how much went in. These questions are like the questions you'll have in the **exam**, so you can **get used to** what you're meant to do and how much you should write.

If you're **not sure** about any of the answers, have another read of the section and then **try again**. **Tick off** each question when you get it right. For the last question there are **extra marks** available for your **spelling**, **punctuation** and **grammar**, so make sure your writing is accurate and that you check through it when you're done.

Let's start you off gently with 1 mark multiple choice questions.

1) Which of the following means preventing pregnancy?
   a) Conception   b) Cohabitation   c) Contraception   d) Conscience ☑

2) Which of the following describes when an unmarried couple live together?
   a) Sex outside of marriage   b) Cohabitation   c) Heterosexuality   d) Promiscuity ☑

3) Which of the following is the term for being married to more than one person?
   a) Procreation   b) Adultery   c) Arranged marriage   d) Polygamy ☑

4) Which of the following is the phrase for the traditional view of men and women's roles?
   a) Gender discrimination   b) Same and equal   c) Separate but equal   d) Gender stereotypes ☑

These questions are worth 2 marks, so you need to write down two brief points.

5) Give two religious beliefs about sexual relationships. ☑

6) Give two religious beliefs about homosexuality. ☑

7) Give two religious beliefs about the significance of procreation. ☑

8) Give two religious beliefs about women's roles. ☑

If you want top marks, you'll need to make sure your answers are well-developed for these questions —
they're worth 4 marks. Make sure your writing is well-organised and accurate so your points are clear.

9) Explain two contrasting beliefs in British society today about promiscuity. ☑

10) Explain two contrasting beliefs in British society today about the nuclear family model. ☑

11) Explain two similar religious beliefs about women in work. ☑

For this question, you must refer to the main religious tradition in the UK and Islam.
This question is worth 4 marks.

12) Explain two contrasting religious beliefs about sex outside of marriage. ☑

And add 1 more — these are worth 5 marks. Your should refer to religious teachings or sacred texts.

13) Explain two religious beliefs about same-sex marriage. ☑

14) Explain two religious beliefs about divorce. ☑

15) Explain two religious beliefs about children's responsibilities towards their parents. ☑

16) Explain two religious beliefs about non-traditional families. ☑

This is the big one you've been waiting for — it's worth 12 marks and another 3 for SPaG.
You'll always be given a list like the one below of things you have to include.
Use it to plan and structure your answer before you start the essay.
It's worth noting down a list of arguments for and against so you're clear on what you need to write about.

17) 'Marriage is a lifelong union between one man and one woman.'
    Evaluate this statement.
    Your answer should include the following:
    • religious arguments that support the statement
    • religious arguments that disagree with the statement
    • a conclusion
    You can also include non-religious points of view in your answer.

    Take a look at the 'Do Well in Your Exam' section — it gives advice on writing essays. ☑

Theme A — Relationships and Families

The Origins of the Universe

Christianity & Islam

No one saw exactly how the **Earth** came to be like it is... but science and religion both have their **theories**.

Scientific arguments — there are two main types

1 Cosmological theories — how the Universe began

Chief amongst these is the **Big Bang** theory. It says that the Universe began in an **explosion** of matter and energy. Matter from this explosion eventually formed stars, planets and **everything** else. The Universe still seems to be expanding — important **evidence** for this theory.

2 Evolutionary theories — how living things changed

Charles Darwin argued that life on Earth originated from simple cells. Life **evolved** (gradually changed) over millions of years into a huge variety of forms, and those **best adapted survived** — 'survival of the fittest'. According to this theory, people evolved from **apes**, not Adam and Eve.

Non-religious people look to science for answers. They believe that the universe and human life came about by **chance**. They say that since people evolved from **apes**, they can't have been created by God.

Religions have their own ideas about all this...

Some religious people believe **only** in the stories written in **scriptures**.

Others believe that science tells them how the world was created, but religion explains why. They believe that God **caused** the Big Bang, and evolution is the way he made humans.

✝ Genesis chapter 1 says God created everything over **six days**. On the seventh day he **rested**. Genesis chapters 1 and 2 describe how God created **people** in **his image**, and made **woman** from **man** (see p.5).

Some Christians believe the Bible gives a **literal** account of what happened. People who disagree with evolution claim there's a lack of proof backing up the theory — **fossils** don't show the **full process** of evolution.

Lots of Christians view the creation story as **symbolic** and also believe in scientific theories.

The Big Bang theory was actually first put forward by a Roman Catholic priest, Georges Lemaître, so religion and science don't have to be completely separate.

"Collaboration between religion and science is mutually beneficial..." *General Synod of the Church of England, 2010*

Many Christians believe that science and religious ideas can exist in **harmony**. Both the Church of England and the Roman Catholic Church have recognised the **benefits** of the two working together.

"Evolution in nature does not conflict with the notion of Creation..." *Pope Francis, Pontifical Academy of Sciences, October 27 2014*

☪ The Muslim creation story is **similar** to that in Genesis:

"It is Allah who created the heavens and the earth and whatever is between them in six days." *Qur'an 32:4*

The Qur'an says Allah *"began the creation of man from clay"* (Qur'an 32:7) and **breathed** life and a **soul** into the first man, Adam — and all humans **descend** from him.

Some see the descriptions of **creation** in the Qur'an as agreeing with **science**. E.g. this quote could be seen to support the **Big Bang theory**.

"Have those who disbelieved not considered that the heavens and the earth were a joined entity, and We separated them..." *Qur'an 21:30*

No monkeying around now, there's a lot to learn here...

Jot down as many beliefs about the origins of the universe as you can for each religion.

General	# The Environment and Stewardship

Religious believers think people should look after the environment because it was created by God.

The world is a way for God to reveal his presence

Many believers **appreciate** the world and what's in it because it is **God's creation**. They feel that he reveals himself constantly in the world through **experiences** that inspire **awe** and **wonder**, where someone can feel God's presence.

But people **don't** always take good **care** of the world we live in...

> For example, a beautiful sunset, a wild sea or a butterfly's wing might convince someone there must be a creator.

Humans have damaged the environment

Global Warming

- Gases in the atmosphere, called 'greenhouse gases', help keep the Earth **warm**.
- Over the past century, the amount of greenhouse gas in the atmosphere has **increased**, and measurements show that the Earth has **got hotter**. This is called **global warming**. Higher temperatures can affect **global weather patterns** an cause ice to **melt**. Ice melting causes **sea levels** to **rise**, which could lead to flooding in low-lying areas.
- It is mainly caused by the fuels used to generate energy, like **oil**, **coal** and **gas**.

Natural Resources

A **natural resource** is anything found naturally that's **useful** to humans.

- The Earth's population is increasing and people use more raw materials and more energy every year. If people carry on like this, many natural resources will eventually **run out**.
- Fertile land for growing crops is also rapidly declining. Each year, overgrazing and irresponsible farming methods turn more fertile land into desert.

Pollution

Pollution from chemicals can **contaminate** the environment.

- **Sewage** and **chemicals** can pollute lakes, rivers and seas. These pollutants **harm** the plants and animals that live in and around the water, including humans.
- People use **toxic chemicals** for farming. They also bury **nuclear waste** underground, and dump a lot of **household** and **industrial waste** in landfill sites. The toxic chemicals can kill plants and animals, and cause cancer in humans.
- **Smoke** and **gases** from vehicles and industry can pollute the **air**, cause health problems in humans and damage the **ozone layer**.

The Environment and Stewardship

There are many ways to tackle environmental problems

Many people, both religious and non-religious, work to reduce and repair the harm caused to the environment. They think that it's important to look after the planet for future generations.

> There's a limit to the Earth's resources, so many people believe it's important to be able to manage the resources currently available and to find alternative, sustainable options too.

Lots of people try to be environmentally friendly by recycling things like paper and plastic.	They may also take public transport or walk to cut down on pollution caused by vehicle fumes and to use less fuel.	Some also campaign to better inform others about the damage being done to the environment and how to live more sustainably.

Christians and Muslims believe in looking after the environment

Many religious believers feel it's their **duty** to look after the environment.
God gave people the Earth, but expects them to **care** for it — this idea is called **stewardship**.

CHRISTIANITY	ISLAM
• God spoke of humanity's power over nature: "...rule over the fish in the sea and the birds in the sky, over the livestock and all the wild animals..." *Genesis 1:26 NIV* This power is known as dominion. Some people think it means humans can use the environment however they want. • God made Christians stewards of the environment: "The Lord God took the man and put him in the Garden of Eden to work it and take care of it." *Genesis 2:15 NIV* • Christians have no right to abuse God's creation, and they have a responsibility to protect it: "humanity's dominion cannot be understood as licence to abuse, spoil, squander or destroy what God has made..." *Christian Declaration on Nature, Assisi 1986* • Everything is interdependent (everything depends on everything else), so driving species of animal or plant to extinction, or harming the planet, eventually ends up harming people. • The damage humans do to the environment clashes with their role as stewards. Christian organisations such as CAFOD, Christian Aid and Tearfund are concerned with putting this responsibility into practice. They put pressure on governments and industry to think more about how people are abusing the planet.	• The Earth is a product of the love of Allah, so Muslims should treat it with love. • Muslims have been appointed khalifah (vice-regents or trustees) of the Earth. This is the idea that while they're on Earth they should take responsibility for the world (stewardship), and make it the sort of place Allah wants it to be. They might carry out this duty by being careful with the resources they use, and encouraging others to take care of the environment too. • At the Day of Judgement questions will be asked of Muslims. They will be required to answer for any ill-treatment of the planet and its resources. • The Prophet Muhammad (called Allah's Apostle here) said that planting a tree is a good, charitable deed: "Allah's Apostle said, 'There is none amongst the Muslims who plants a tree or sows seeds, and then a bird, or a person or an animal eats from it, but is regarded as a charitable gift for him.'" *Sahih al-Bukhari 39:513*

Look after the environment — it's the natural thing to do...

Define stewardship, then write a few points about how people might carry it out.

Christianity & Islam	**Animal Rights**

You need to know about **religious views** on animal experimentation and using animals for food.

Animal experimentation and vegetarianism are key issues

Animals are sometimes used... **...to test products** used by humans or for **medical experiments**

- Some people see this as **cruel**.
- Others look at the issue in a **utilitarian** way. They argue that animal testing is **acceptable** if it could help many people, even if animals suffer.

...for food 🍗
- Some say that humans are **built** to **consume meat**.
- Other people argue that hurting animals is wrong, so it's better to be **vegetarian** or **vegan**.

> **utilitarianism**
> *the idea that decisions should be made based on what has the best balance of good and bad outcomes*

Christians have different beliefs on how animals should be treated ✝

Due to **different interpretations** of the Bible, there isn't just one Christian belief about animal rights:

👍 Views in FAVOUR of animal rights	👎 Views AGAINST
🐑 **Stewardship** means caring for God's creatures and treating them with **kindness**: *"The righteous care for the needs of their animals." Proverbs 12:10 NIV*	🐑 **Dominion** gives humans the right to do what they want with animals.
It's always **wrong** to cause **suffering** to animals to increase scientific knowledge, particularly since medicines don't always have the same effect on humans as they do on animals.	🐑 **Only human life** is **sacred**, as only humans were created in the **image of God**.
🐑 Some denominations, e.g. the **Society of Friends** (Quakers), are **against** any ill-treatment of animals.	🍗 The **Bible** talks about eating meat, so it's fine.

MIXED views

- Animal testing is tolerated only if it **benefits** mankind, and the animals' **suffering** is considered:

  > *"Medical and scientific experimentation on animals is a morally acceptable practice if it remains within reasonable limits and contributes to caring for or saving human lives. It is contrary to human dignity to cause animals to suffer or die needlessly." Catechism of the Catholic Church, 2417-2418*

- Christianity has no specific **food laws** so **vegetarianism** (not eating meat) and **veganism** (not eating or using any animal products) are matters for **individuals** to decide about.

Islam teaches that animals should never be mistreated

The idea of **khalifah** affects how Muslims treat animals (see p.49). Animals are part of **Allah's creation**, which Muslims are entrusted to **look after**. Cruelty to animals is **forbidden**, as is their use simply for **pleasure**.

> **"It is Allah who made for you the grazing animals... you eat."** *Qur'an 40:79*

- Muslims believe in showing **compassion** for all creatures — animals must be **slaughtered humanely** for the meat to be **halal** (Arabic for 'allowed').
- Muslims will generally only allow animal testing if it is done to produce genuine medical **advances** for humans. The animals should be treated humanely, and **no unnecessary pain** should be inflicted on them.

> **"Allah's Apostle said, 'Whoever keeps a dog, one Qirat of the reward of his good deeds is deducted daily, unless the dog is used for guarding a farm or cattle.'"** *Sahih al-Bukhari 39:515*

 REVISION TASK

Animal rights shouldn't be left out...
Summarise what each religion teaches about animal rights. Try to mention sacred texts too.

Abortion and Euthanasia

Make sure you know the views of **non-religious** people, **Christians** and **Muslims** on abortion and euthanasia.

Abortion and euthanasia are legal under certain conditions

There are different **types** of euthanasia and different **laws** in the UK for abortion and euthanasia.
The **table** below tells you all you need to know about this:

Term	Definition	Treatment by UK law
abortion	*when a foetus is removed prematurely from the womb before it can survive*	**Legal** in the UK and can take place until the **24th week** of pregnancy. Abortions can take place **after** this time if there's a **danger** to the **health** of the mother or foetus.
euthanasia	*killing someone to relieve suffering (often from an incurable disease)*	**Varies** depending on if the euthanasia is **passive** or **active**.
active euthanasia	*helping someone who wants to end their own suffering to die*	**Illegal** in the **UK**, but legal in some countries, e.g. **Belgium**.
passive euthanasia	*withdrawing medical treatment that might extend someone's life*	**Legal** in the **UK**.

Abortion and euthanasia are controversial issues

Many atheists support abortion as it gives women **control** over what happens to their **bodies**.
Humanists **prioritise** quality of life over sustaining life, and look at the **impact** on the **woman** first.

HOWEVER... there is some **debate** surrounding the **time limit** on abortions:

 Since some babies born **prematurely** at 24 weeks or less **survive**, some feel that the **timeframe** for abortions should be **shortened**.

 Others feel that there **shouldn't** be a time limit on abortions at all.

There is even more of a **divide** in opinions when it comes to **euthanasia**:

 Some support it when a person will **die** from an illness or where they are suffering from an **incurable** illness. They feel that ending someone's **suffering** through euthanasia is the **kindest** thing to do.

 However, some people fear that **legalising** euthanasia would potentially lead to people feeling **pressured** into it. Some also feel that **doctors** should work to **protect** lives, not the opposite.

With abortion and euthanasia, many people look at the factors of each particular case — this is known as **situation ethics**. They think **decisions** should be made based on what is best in **each situation**, not by following **rules** that should apply to **every instance**.

Christianity | Abortion and Euthanasia

Christians are generally against abortion and euthanasia

All life is created by God.	➤	As God's creation, all life **belongs** to God and is therefore **holy**.	➤	This is the **'sanctity of life'** argument.

Based on this **'sanctity of life'** argument, many religious people (Christians and Muslims — see next page) believe that people **don't** have the **right** to **interfere** with when life **ends**, or to **prevent new life**. Other people take into consideration a person's **quality of life** (how **able** they are to live a **normal** life).

	Christian views AGAINST...	MIXED views on...

...abortion	• Abortion is **undesirable** as God *"created mankind in his own image"* (Genesis 1:27 NIV).
	
	  • The **Roman Catholic Church** goes so far as to say that abortion is **murder**, as it teaches that human life **starts** as soon as the egg is fertilised at **conception**.
	
	  "...all direct abortion... [is] to be absolutely excluded as lawful means of regulating the number of children." Humanae Vitae, section 14
	
	• Abortion is wrong because God **cares** about all of His **children**.
	
	• Some Christian writings (e.g. the **Didache**, a 2nd century manual of Christian teaching) are quite specifically **against** abortion.
		• Abortion is **permissible** in **certain circumstances**, such as when the pregnancy puts the **mother's life** at **risk**. The **life** of the unborn child **cannot** be valued **above** the mother.
		
		• Allowing a woman to **choose** is a way of showing **Christian compassion** — regardless of whether or not they agree with the woman's choice or not.
		
		• The Bible **doesn't** actually mention abortion, but it connects **life** with **breath**, e.g. in the creation of Adam — so it could be argued that the foetus is only **alive** when it breathes.

...euthanasia	• **Roman Catholics** believe that **anything** that intentionally causes death is **wrong**. So even those who are **unlikely** to recover should be kept **alive**.
	
	  "...an act or omission which... causes death in order to eliminate suffering constitutes a murder..." Catechism of the Catholic Church, 2277
	
	• Euthanasia goes against the commandment *"You shall not murder"*. Only **God** should **decide** when a person's life **ends**, as he initially gave them life.
	
	• Suffering is **part of life**. Job was made to **suffer** by Satan, but **refused** to **end** his life:
	
	  "Shall we accept good from God, and not trouble?" Job 2:10 NIV
	
	• Euthanasia could be seen to **ruin** the natural course of death, when a **soul** starts to make its way to God.
	
	• Many Christians feel they must **care** for sick people, and euthanasia **goes against** this. Local churches often have links with **hospices** — a hospice is a place where **terminally ill** people can be well cared for. This allows a person to feel **valued** as they reach the end of their life.
		• The use of **'extraordinary treatment'** (e.g. life-support machines which are keeping someone alive **artificially**) is **not always** the best approach — the **easing** of **suffering** through **passive euthanasia** is a way of demonstrating **Christian compassion**.
		
		  • However, many only agree with euthanasia if the dying person **chooses** it for themselves.
		
		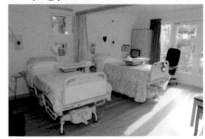
		
		• Anglican denominations are **against active euthanasia**. However, they agree that terrible distress should not be suffered **at all costs**, and that death may be considered a **blessing** rather than continuing life-extending treatment. They argue that a person's **quality of life** must also be considered.

Abortion and Euthanasia

Islam *allows abortion before ensoulment* in some circumstances

The Qur'an teaches that people's lives are **sacred** —
this is the 'sanctity of life' argument (see previous page).
This means that abortion is **generally** seen as wrong:

> "whoever kills a soul... it is as if he had slain mankind entirely." *Qur'an 5:32*

> "And do not kill your children... We provide for them and for you. Indeed, their killing is ever a great sin." *Qur'an 17:31*

But there are **two** circumstances in which abortion is **permissible**:

1 **Before ensoulment** of the foetus:
Muslims believe ensoulment occurs after **120 days**, so abortion can be allowed before this if the baby would be born with a serious **defect**.

> **ensoulment**
> *when a foetus gets its soul*

2 When the **mother's** life is in **danger**:
The **potential** life in the womb is **not** as **important** as the **actual** life of the mother. It is only in this situation that an abortion is allowed after 120 days.

> Some Muslim women argue that they should be **free** to **choose** what happens to their **bodies**.

BUT

> Those that disagree claim that Qur'an 81:8-9 says **unborn children** will want to know **why** they were **killed**.

Muslims are usually *against euthanasia*

Euthanasia is seen as **wrong** by most Muslims, because their lives are **Allah's**. Muslims believe that Allah has a **plan** for every living person — he has decided **how long** each person will live on this Earth, and they do not have the right to **interfere** with that plan.

> "O you who have believed, seek help through patience and prayer. Indeed, Allah is with the patient." *Qur'an 2:153*

> "...when disaster strikes them, [they] say, 'Indeed we belong to Allah, and indeed to Him we will return.' Those are the ones upon whom are blessings from their Lord and mercy." *Qur'an 2:156-157*

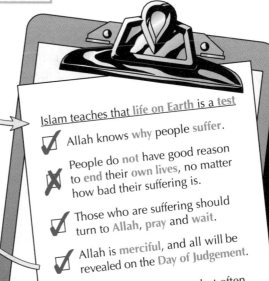

Islam teaches that life on Earth is a test
- ☑ Allah knows why people suffer.
- ☒ People do not have good reason to end their own lives, no matter how bad their suffering is.
- ☑ Those who are suffering should turn to Allah, pray and wait.
- ☑ Allah is merciful, and all will be revealed on the Day of Judgement.

Muslims support hospices, but often they try to look after the ill person at home to allow them to be surrounded by family and friends. However, doctors can stop 'unnecessary' treatment when a patient has no hope of improvement.

 EXAM TIP

The last few pages have covered a lot of information

...so go back over them if you need to. You need to be able to talk about views on abortion and euthanasia in Christianity and Islam, so make sure you know the differences between them.

The Afterlife

Every religion in the world has something to say about **death** — and what comes **after** it.

Most religions teach that there is an afterlife

- Some religions teach that the soul is **rewarded** or **punished** for the **actions** of the person on Earth.
- Others believe the soul is **reincarnated**.
- Christians and Muslims believe that life on Earth isn't **everything** — a **better life** awaits them. It's still **important** though, and is **preparation** for the afterlife.

> **afterlife** (life after death) a different kind of existence for the soul after the body has died

CHRISTIANS believe Jesus's **resurrection** shows that there's life after death.

Christianity teaches that people go to heaven or hell, depending on how God judges their actions — trying to live life according to Christian teachings and believing in Jesus will allow them to receive God's grace and go to heaven.

Catholics believe that some go to Purgatory — a place where sins are paid for before going to heaven (see p.8).

> "He was put to death in the body but **made alive in the Spirit.**" *1 Peter 3:18 NIV*

> "And God raised us up with Christ and seated us with him in the heavenly realms in Christ Jesus... For it is by grace you have been saved..." *Ephesians 2:6-8 NIV*

> "...one who had repented, believed, and done righteousness, it is promised by Allah that he will be among the successful." *Qur'an 28:67*

MUSLIMS believe the afterlife means going to jannah (paradise) or jahannam (hell). After a person dies, their soul goes to barzakh to await judgement (see p.30).

On Yawm ad-Din (the Day of Judgement), everyone's actions will be judged. Muslims believe Allah *"...will assemble you for the Day of Resurrection..."* (Qur'an 45:26). Those who Allah deems good go to jannah, and the bad to jahannam.

Many **NON-RELIGIOUS** people believe that when you die, that's it — you **cease to exist**. There isn't any **concrete evidence** that there is life after death, so the **logical** answer is that it **doesn't exist**.

Believing in an afterlife is just a way of **helping** people deal with **death** — the idea gives **comfort**.

The idea of an afterlife is used by religions to put **pressure** on people to **follow** their teachings and **live** their lives in a certain way.

There are many **arguments** used by both **religious** and **non-religious** people to **support** life after death:

The **paranormal** (things science can't explain, which are thought to have a spiritual cause, e.g. **ghosts**) is sometimes used as evidence. Some people (**mediums**) claim they can **talk** to the **dead**.

Some people claim to have evidence of **reincarnation** (they lived a previous life, died, and were reborn in a new body). Lots of research has been carried out with young **children** who claim to remember **past lives**.

People say they've had a **near-death** or **out-of-body experience** where they've spoken to long-dead **family members**.

Some believe there must be **more** after **life on Earth**. They might see going to heaven or paradise as a **reward** for people who've been **good** all their lives — it must exist to **compensate** for the **unfairness** of life on Earth.

It might not seem like it now, but there is life after exams

Explain two reasons religious people believe in life after death. Use sacred text references. [5]

Revision Summary

Those were some pretty big issues that you've just read about — now let's see how much you can remember. These questions will let you get a feel for how the exam will be, and how much writing is involved.

If there's anything you can't answer, go back through the section and have another go when you've re-read it. For the last question there are extra marks for spelling, punctuation and grammar, so check your writing carefully.

Getting the ball rolling with some 1 mark questions — they're even multiple choice.

1) Which of the following is the theory that humans evolved from apes?
   a) The Big Bang   b) Reincarnation   c) Ensoulment   d) Evolution ☐

2) Which of the following is the idea that believers must look after God's creation?
   a) Veganism   b) Dominion   c) Stewardship   d) Halal ☐

3) Which of the following words means to terminate a pregnancy?
   a) Abortion   b) Euthanasia   c) Conception   d) Purgatory ☐

4) Which of the following is the approach of making decisions by looking at each individual case?
   a) Utilitarianism   b) Situation ethics   c) Humanism   d) Compassion ☐

Let's make things a little trickier. 2 marks = 2 short points.

5) Give two religious beliefs about how people might experience God's presence through the natural world. ☐

6) Give two examples of what religious people could do to protect the environment. ☐

7) Give two religious beliefs about dominion. ☐

8) Give two religious beliefs about eating meat. ☐

Moving up to 4 marks. Make two points, but this time develop them further to get an extra mark for each. Talk about the views of one or both religions.

Make sure that you write clearly and organise your answer well for the longer answer questions.

9) Explain two different religious beliefs about how the human race began. ☐

10) Explain two similar religious beliefs about the sanctity of life. ☐

11) Explain two similar religious beliefs about what happens after death. ☐

For this question, you must refer to the main religious tradition in the UK and at least one other religious viewpoint. There are 4 marks available for this question.

12) Explain two contrasting beliefs about animal experimentation in Britain today. ☐

5 marks up for grabs now. You'll need to refer to religious texts for top marks.

13) Explain two religious beliefs about how the world was created. ☐

14) Explain two religious beliefs about evolution. ☐

15) Explain two religious beliefs about stewardship. ☐

16) Explain two religious beliefs about abortion. ☐

And last but not least — the 12 mark question (with another 3 marks for SPaG). The question will always come with bullet points that you should include in your answer, so use them to make a plan before you begin. Think about arguments in favour of and against the statement, and pack your answer full of information.

17) 'Euthanasia can be the most compassionate way to help someone who is terminally ill.'
   Evaluate this statement.
   Your answer should include the following:
   • religious arguments that support the statement
   • religious arguments that disagree with the statement
   • a conclusion
   You can also include non-religious points of view in your answer.

Turn to the 'Do Well in Your Exam' section for more about writing essays. ☐

General, Christianity & Islam	**Design and Causation**

The belief that God **created** the world is an **important part** of **many religions**, and often strengthens **faith**.

Different people *believe for different reasons*

- About **84%** of the **global population** belongs to a religion (source: Pew Research Center).
- The rest don't have specific religious beliefs, or have **no spiritual beliefs**.

There are **various reasons** why people might **FOLLOW** or **REJECT** religion:

FOLLOW
- People want to find out **why** life is as it is. Some people are convinced the '**design**' or '**causation**' arguments explain this.
- Some are drawn to the **purpose**, **structure** and **comfort** religion provides, or simply by the desire to have something to **believe**.
- Some people's faith is strengthened by the feelings they experience during **worship** and as part of a religious **community**.
- People brought up by religious **parents** or in a religious **community** are more likely to believe in a god.

REJECT
- There's **no proof** there's a god.
- Religion causes too much **strife** between people.
- The **evil** in the world shows there's no god.

- **Atheists reject** the idea of a **divine being**.
- **Agnostics** believe it's **impossible** to know **either way** for **certain**.

The design argument: *'The Universe* must have had a designer'

- Belief that God **created** the universe is a **central** part of **belief in God** — not only does the Universe's existence **prove** God's existence, but believers think it shows some of his **characteristics**, e.g. his **power**.
- Many Christians and Muslims believe a god **exists** because of '**design**' arguments. The idea is that the **intricate workings** of the **universe** can't have come about by **chance**. There must have been some kind of **designer** — a **god**. The Bible and the Qur'an **support** this argument:

> ✝ "...since the creation of the world God's invisible qualities — his eternal power and divine nature — have been clearly seen, being understood from what has been made." *Romans 1:20 NIV*

> ☪ "In the creation of the heavens and earth, and the alternation of the night and the day ... and ... the winds and the clouds ... are signs for a people who use reason." *Qur'an 2:164*

- Some think aspects of **nature** support this idea. For example, **snowflakes** form **complex** shapes that are **unique** to each **individual** snowflake.

 William Paley's **watchmaker argument** says that if you came across an intricate **watch**, you wouldn't think it was made **by chance** — you would assume it had been **designed**. The same must be true of **complex structures** in **nature**.

- **Scientists** say the **conditions** that led to the **creation** of the **universe** and **life** were extremely **specific**. The **fine-tuning argument** says this shows there was a **designer** — they couldn't have occurred by **chance**.

Some people aren't convinced *by these arguments*

- In **2009**, a survey found **37%** of people in **Britain** thought **evolution** was 'beyond reasonable doubt'.

Charles Darwin explained how species **developed** by **adapting** themselves to the **conditions** around them through '**survival of the fittest**'. **Species** or **individuals** that have **characteristics** that are **beneficial** for survival are **more likely** to live, while those that aren't well-adapted are **more likely to die** out. This helps to explain how species have **developed** their characteristics through **time** — known as **evolution**.

Darwin didn't see evolution as conclusive proof against God's existence.

- Followers of religion, including Christians and Muslims, have **differing** views on evolution:

> Evolution **doesn't** contradict the **design argument** — God or Allah must have '**designed**' evolution.

vs.

> It's a struggle to **reconcile** evolution with the belief that God created **humans** in his own image — it seems **unlikely** he would have done so by **slowly evolving** humans from **apes**.

- Non-religious people may also hold a range of views, for example:

> God **created** the universe but has not had any **further involvement** with it.

 **vs.**

> There's **no evidence** the '**designer**' and **creator** still exists.

Design and Causation

Ideas about **causation** have been used over the **centuries** as evidence that a divine being **exists**.

Causation: 'There must have been a first cause'

The **First Cause** argument, also known as the **cosmological argument**, is founded on a **chain of logic**. Everything that **happens** is **caused** by **something else**. An event **now** was caused by an **earlier** event, that was caused by an **even earlier** event, etc. If you trace this **chain** back in time, there are **two** possibilities:

1 The chain goes back **forever** — i.e. the universe has **always** existed, it's **eternal**.

2 You eventually reach a **starting point** — an **uncaused** cause or 'First Cause'.

Some think the 'First Cause' was **God**, as only he is **eternal** and has enough **power** to create the universe.

Religious figures **have theorised** about the First Cause

ISLAM

The Muslim theologian **al-Ghazali** believed that **everything** that starts to exist was **caused to exist**. The **universe** started to exist, so it had a **cause** — Allah. The focus on the universe having **started** to exist (i.e. not being **infinite**) is a **key part** of the theory, known as the **kalam cosmological argument**. Al-Ghazali believed the **universe** was made up of **chains of events** that Allah had **predetermined**.

CHRISTIANITY

Thomas Aquinas, a 13th century monk, developed Five Ways to prove God exists. They've been influential in Christianity. Three of them have a similar logic to the 'First Cause' theory:

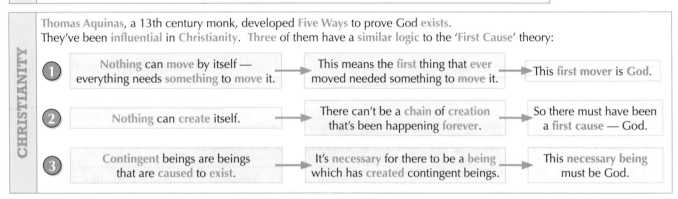

1 Nothing can move by itself — everything needs something to move it. → This means the first thing that ever moved needed something to move it. → This first mover is God.

2 Nothing can create itself. → There can't be a chain of creation that's been happening forever. → So there must have been a first cause — God.

3 Contingent beings are beings that are caused to exist. → It's necessary for there to be a being which has created contingent beings. → This necessary being must be God.

There are differing opinions on the First Cause argument

Many Christians and Muslims use the First Cause argument as **evidence** there is a **god**, often in **combination** with **accounts** from the **scriptures** and the **design** argument. However, some people question its **logic**:

The argument **contradicts** itself — it says **everything** has to have a **cause**, but then says there must be an **event** that didn't have a **cause** — the first cause.

There's **no evidence** that if there is a **first cause**, it has to be a **divine being** — a god.

Even if a god was the **first cause**, it doesn't mean they **still** exist now. It also doesn't give any **indication** that the god has the **characteristics** of the **Christian** or **Muslim** god.

Sacred texts **are used as evidence** that God created the world

✝ **Christian** teachings on **creation** are taken from Genesis 1, which says God created **everything**. The process took **6 days**, and people **didn't evolve** from **apes**, but **descended** from **Adam** and **Eve**.

☪ The **Qur'an** says that **Allah** created the world. It says Allah made Adam from **clay** and breathed **life** and a **soul** into him — and that all humans **descend** from **Adam**.

"Allah constructed it" *Qur'an 79:27*

Some believers take the descriptions in the sacred texts **literally**, e.g. some Christians accept the account given in Genesis.

Others see the accounts as **symbolic** — they still believe God is the creator, but they look to science to explain how it all happened

Blimey, it's enough to make your head spin...

It's a good idea to read these two pages again to get them in your head — they're pretty complex.

Christianity & Islam	Miracles

As well as learning **both religions'** beliefs, make sure you can compare **Christian** and **non-religious** views.

Many believe miracles prove there is a God

- Christianity and Islam both involve some **belief** in **miracles**, though to **differing** extents.
- These include events in their **scriptures**, though some people believe miracles also happen **nowadays**.

> **miracles**
> *seemingly inexplicable events, such as people with apparently incurable illnesses being healed*

- **Others** argue that the miracles in religious texts should be interpreted **symbolically** rather than literally.
- Beliefs about miracles include:

> They offer **proof** there is a god because they go **against** the laws of **nature** — only God would have the **power** to do so.

> They also show God's **benevolence**, as many miracles are **beneficial**, e.g. **healing** someone who is ill.

> Healing people also shows that God can **decide** who **lives** or **dies**.

Christians read stories of miracles in the New Testament

- Jesus performed **miracles** to show he had the **power** of **God**, and to show the **importance** of **faith**.

> Examples include the **feeding of the 5000** and **healing a blind man** — see p.92 for more detail.

- Christians believe the **birth** and **resurrection** of Jesus were **miracles** in their **own right** (see p.9-10).

Muslims believe the Qur'an is a miracle in itself

- Muslims believe the Qur'an is a **miracle** — the **direct** word of Allah, with a **style** that's **impossible** to **copy**.

> **"If mankind ... gathered ... to produce the like of this Qur'an, they could not."** *Qur'an 17:88*

> Some believe the Qur'an contains **'scientific miracles'** — it describes facts discovered **centuries** later, such as an account of how the **human embryo** develops (Qur'an 23:13-14) or a reference to the **Big Bang** (Qur'an 21:30).

> Some **disagree**, saying the descriptions aren't **detailed** enough to be **certain**.

- Many Muslims think that the **prophets** performed **miracles** in order to show they had been **sent by God**.

Some people don't believe in miracles

- Some believers prefer to focus on **God** and living their life in a **moral way** rather than on **miracles**.
- **Atheists** and **humanists** don't believe in miracles. They believe they can either be explained **scientifically**, or are **fakes** or **misunderstandings**.

> For example, they might explain someone being **cured** of a **terminal** disease by saying they must have been **misdiagnosed**, or the hope of a **religious figure** healing them had **stimulated** their **recovery** — called the **placebo effect**, this also happens when people are given **fake pills**.

- It can be a matter of **perspective** — a **religious** person might seek a **miraculous** explanation for something **atheists** and **humanists** would call a **coincidence**, e.g. something happening **soon** after you **prayed** for it.

Don't rely on a miracle to pass your exam — revise well...

... and do exam questions. Miraculously, we've got one here:

Explain two contrasting beliefs about miracles.
Refer to the main religious tradition of Great Britain as well as non-religious beliefs. [4]

Theme C — The Existence of God and Revelation

Revelation

For **nature as revelation** and **visions**, you need to be able to compare **Christian** and **non-religious** views.

Revelation is how God's presence is revealed

- It's **difficult** to **conclusively prove** God **exists**. So Christians and Muslims look for **evidence** to reveal God's **presence**. They believe he is **revealed** in **different** ways, including through the **scriptures**, the **world** around us and **religious experiences**.

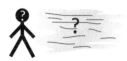

- Revelation doesn't just involve knowing God **exists**, but also what he's **like** and what he **expects** of people. Revelations can **give rise to** or **strengthen** people's **belief** in a god.

- There are **two** main types of **revelation** — **special** revelation and **general** revelation:

Special Revelation	General Revelation
• **Special revelations** are revelations to **specific** people, e.g. **Allah's** revelation of the Qur'an to **Muhammad**. • They include revelations through **prophethood** (written down as **scriptures**), **visions** and **miracles** (see p.58). • They're **direct** and **personal**, so they can be **powerful** experiences. However, they're hard to **prove**. • Some think they **still** occur today, while others **disagree**.	• **General revelations** are revelations **available** to **everyone**. They're more **indirect** and therefore have to be **interpreted**. • Many think the **world** is an **example** of **general revelation**. Believers think God **created** the world, so it **proves** he exists. • Many think our **conscience** proves God exists, as people all over the world have **similar morals**, e.g. that **killing** is wrong. God must have **created** this within **every person**.

The scriptures are important revelations

- Christians and Muslims believe God's **nature** and **will** are revealed in their **holy books**. Many believe they were either **inspired** by **God** or came **directly** from him. They contain **knowledge** of **God** and the **faith**.

- Most religious people believe that **all** or **parts** of them were **special revelations**, as they were revealed to **specific prophets**. In their **written** form, they also have some **features** of **general revelation** — they are **available** to **everyone**, all the **time**, and they need to be **interpreted** to be **understood**.

The Bible	
• The Bible is a **collection** of books written by **various** authors. • Some Christians think the authors were **inspired** and **guided** by God as they **wrote**, but he didn't **directly** reveal it to them. • The **New Testament** describes Jesus's **life** — Jesus is seen as the **completion** of God's **revelation** to people. • Jesus is seen as the 'new covenant' — he **died** for people's **sins**, but in return **people** should **worship** God.	✝ "God spoke to our ancestors through the prophets at many times and in various ways, but in these last days he has spoken to us by his son" *Hebrews 1:1-2 NIV*

The Qur'an	
• Muslims believe **Allah** revealed the **Qur'an directly** to Muhammad. • It's a **fully accurate** record of Allah's **final** revelation to **humankind**. • Allah gave **earlier** revelations to prophets such as **Musa** (Moses) and **Isa** (Jesus) but the texts have been **altered**.	

- Many **atheists** and **humanists** think the scriptures depict their authors' **ideas** about **God**, and that many of the events in them **didn't occur**. They may see these ancient texts as largely **irrelevant** to **life today**.

Revelations show God's nature

- **Christians** and **Muslims** have **similar** beliefs about many of God's **characteristics**. He is:

• **omniscient** — all-knowing • **infinite** — he has no limits • **omnipotent** — all-powerful • **transcendent** — beyond this world • **immanent** — involved in the world	• **eternal** — he has always existed and always will • the **creator** and **sustainer** of the universe — he made it and keeps it going • **all-loving** — infinite in his mercy and compassion and completely **good** • **personal** — believers can have a **relationship** with God, e.g. through **prayer** • **impersonal** — others see him as **distant** from people as he **rarely** acts in the world

- The scriptures can show God's **characteristics**. E.g. these verses suggest to believers that God is **personal**:

 "He is with you wherever you are" *Qur'an 57:4*

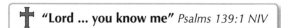 "Lord ... you know me" *Psalms 139:1 NIV*

- Believers think God shows his **compassion** through his **intervention** in the world — e.g. showing people how to live a **better life** through the **prophets** in both faiths, and through **Jesus** as Messiah in Christian belief.

Theme C — The Existence of God and Revelation

General & Christianity	# Revelation

Some see nature as revelation

- Christians and Muslims believe **God** created the **world**, so it **shows** God **exists**.

- Many believers feel that nature provides **numinous** experiences. These are events that inspire **awe** and **wonder**, where someone can feel God's **presence**, e.g. a beautiful **sunset** might convince them there is a **creator**.

  numinous
  spiritual

- **Interventions** in **nature**, e.g. **miracles**, show God's **immanence**. Nature may show God's **transcendence** — he **created** it but isn't **present** in it — as well as other **aspects**:

Characteristics such as God's **intelligence** are revealed through the **complexity** of nature. Nature is often **cruel**, which can be hard to explain. Some believe nature became **cruel** after the **Fall** — when Adam and Eve **sinned**. So nature no longer fully shows what God is **like**.

> "The heavens declare the glory of God; the skies proclaim the work of his hands." *Psalms 19:1 NIV*

> "The beauty of creation reflects the infinite beauty of the Creator." *Catechism of the Catholic Church 341*

Allah created the universe — all **beauty** comes from him as a gift, and can move people to **faith** in its creator. One of the 99 names of Allah is **Al-Musawwir** — The **Shaper** of **Beauty**. The beauty of the **world** shows the beauty of **Allah**.

- **Atheists** and **humanists** don't believe that **nature** reveals **God**. They argue that even aspects of **nature** we don't fully understand, e.g. how animals **navigate** as they **migrate**, will one day be **explained** by **science**.

God can be revealed through religious experiences

Religious experiences are **personal experiences** of God — they're a form of **special revelation**.

- They can take many **forms**, such as:
  - a vision
  - a dream
  - hearing a voice
  - a feeling of ecstasy or peace
  - feelings of being loved, forgiven or guided

- They can take place during **prayer** or **worship**, or at **other times**.

- They can be so **powerful** they **change** the **life** of the person, or they might be more gentle experiences.

- Other religious **believers** may take **inspiration** from someone who's had such an experience. Some people who have had religious experiences become **well known** — see below and the next page.

Visions are a dramatic form of religious experience

- A **vision** is a religious experience in which a person sees something **sacred** — such as an **angel**. **Visions** usually tell the receiver about **God** and his **will**, or about the receiver's **own life**.

- Visions are **direct** and **powerful** forms of religious experience. They often **change** how believers **live** their **lives** — they can **strengthen** people's **faith** or even **induce** them to believe in something they **didn't** believe in **before**. They can convince people that **God exists** — only **he** could have made them **happen**.

There are many examples of visions in Christianity

- Some **visions** are reported in the **Bible**, which gives them **authority**, as they're part of the **scripture**.

The **disciples** saw a vision of Moses and Elijah with Jesus, who was covered in **light** — see Matthew 17:1-13 and p.94.	St Paul was originally named **Saul**. He **persecuted** Christians. One day he saw a **light**, and heard **Jesus** asking why Saul was **persecuting** him. This **transformed** Saul's life — he became **Christian** and spent the rest of his life preaching the **gospel**.

- Other visions of **Mary** or **angels** appeared to people **later**. The Churches confirm if they think they're **authentic**. **Belief** in this type of vision is more **significant** in **Catholicism** than in **Protestant** Christianity.

Joan of Arc was a French peasant. She had **visions** of the **archangel Michael**, among others. These encouraged her to lead **France** against **England** in the **Hundred Years' War**. She was **captured** and **killed** by English allies. The **Catholic Church** declared her a **saint** — Catholics think her visions were **genuine**.	Many Catholics report visions of **Mary**. One example is **Bernadette Soubirous**, who claimed she saw Mary several times in 1858 near **Lourdes** (France). Lourdes is now a popular **pilgrimage** site — many think people can be **healed** by visiting it.

Theme C — The Existence of God and Revelation

Revelation

The Qur'an mentions stories of people who had visions

- The Qur'an includes the story of the angel Jibril (Gabriel) appearing to Maryam (Mary), the mother of Isa (Jesus) — see Qur'an 19:16-22. Jibril told her she would bear a son, even though she was a virgin.
- The angel Jibril appeared to Muhammad while he was meditating in a cave outside Makkah. Muhammad recited the verses Jibril gave to him — these were the first verses of the Qur'an to be revealed.
- There are other examples of seemingly miraculous events or visions in Islam:

> "We have shown clearly the signs to a people who are certain [in faith]." *Qur'an 2:118*

This shows how Allah reveals himself.

Sufi Muslims are Muslim mystics who seek to be filled with knowledge and love of Allah through direct experience of him, which can include visions. This affects them spiritually at a deep level. Sufis can be Sunni or Shi'a, but many Muslims are sceptical of the Sufis' religious experiences.

Many people don't believe in religious experiences

Religious experiences are private, so it's impossible to show proof of them to someone else.
Atheists and humanists don't believe in God, so think religious experiences can be explained in other ways:

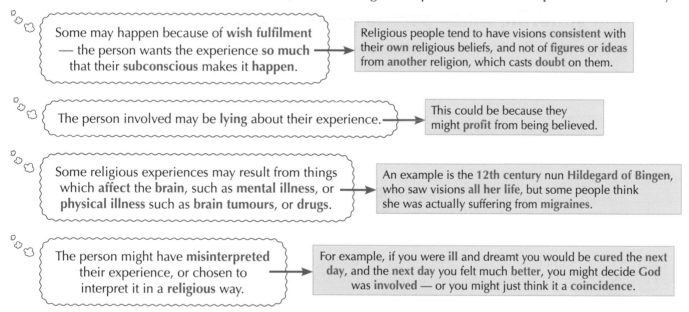

Some may happen because of wish fulfilment — the person wants the experience so much that their subconscious makes it happen.

Religious people tend to have visions consistent with their own religious beliefs, and not of figures or ideas from another religion, which casts doubt on them.

The person involved may be lying about their experience.

This could be because they might profit from being believed.

Some religious experiences may result from things which affect the brain, such as mental illness, or physical illness such as brain tumours, or drugs.

An example is the 12th century nun Hildegard of Bingen, who saw visions all her life, but some people think she was actually suffering from migraines.

The person might have misinterpreted their experience, or chosen to interpret it in a religious way.

For example, if you were ill and dreamt you would be cured the next day, and the next day you felt much better, you might decide God was involved — or you might just think it a coincidence.

Some believers may not believe in these experiences either, particularly ones not written in their sacred text. They might prefer to focus on God and living a good life instead of events which may or may not be true.

> Religious experiences can bring up contradictions in the ideas people have about God. It's hard to understand why, if God is capable of acting in the world, he doesn't do it more often. Miracles (see p.58) show God's power as they break the laws of nature, but this doesn't explain why he doesn't use his power to prevent suffering (see p.62).

EXAM QUESTION

Branches of the same faith may have different views...

...so make sure you revise different opinions, as you'll often be asked to give two contrasting beliefs in the exam. Meanwhile, try this exam-style question:

Explain two religious beliefs about visions. Refer to sacred texts in your answer. [5]

Theme C — The Existence of God and Revelation

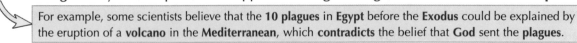

Christianity & Islam — # Arguments Against the Existence of God

Atheists *and humanists* argue there's no evidence

- Many **atheists** and **humanists** don't believe in God because they don't think there's any **evidence** he exists.
- They say **visions** and **miracles** have **scientific** or **straightforward** explanations, and aren't **proof** of a **divine being**. Many such experiences happened a **long time ago**, before science could **explain** them.

> For example, some scientists believe that the **10 plagues** in **Egypt** before the **Exodus** could be explained by the eruption of a **volcano** in the **Mediterranean**, which **contradicts** the belief that **God** sent the **plagues**.

- Atheists and humanists argue that **science** provides **sufficient explanation** for the **origins** of the **universe**.

Many think the Big Bang Theory explains creation

The theory says that the **universe** suddenly **expanded** from an initial state of very high **density** and **temperature** — this event is known as the '**Big Bang**'. **Matter** from this **explosion** eventually formed **stars**, **planets** and **everything else**. There's quite a lot of **evidence** to **back up** this theory.

- However, we **don't** know what **caused** the Big Bang — so many Christians and Muslims argue that it was **God** or **Allah** who **caused** it, which seems to fit with the 'First Cause' argument.
- Some Muslims think the **Qur'an** mentions **Allah** creating the **Big Bang**.

> "...the heavens and the earth were a joined entity ... We separated them and made from water every living thing." *Qur'an 21:30*

Evil and suffering make people doubt there is a God

Christians and **Muslims** may have very **different** views on evil and suffering to **non-religious** people:

> God is **omniscient** (all-knowing), **omnipotent** (all-powerful), and **benevolent** (kind). He knows what **happens** in the world, doesn't want people to **suffer**, and is **powerful** enough to do something about it.

 VS.

> There's a lot of **suffering** in the world, which seems to **contradict** these ideas. It's hard to see how God could **allow** it to happen, so it's doubtful he exists.

> In the scriptures, suffering is often described as **punishment** for people's sins, e.g. God **destroyed** a town of people he considered **sinful**, while **sparing** a few who weren't.

 VS.

> Suffering is **widespread** and affects **everyone**, so **justifying** suffering as **punishment** doesn't make sense. It also doesn't seem to add up because **other animals** suffer too, even though they **can't** be being punished for their sins.

Believers might explain it by saying that humans need to be able to **choose** between **good** and **evil** as a test of their **character** — that's why they have **free will**. Without **bad** things happening, good **can't** exist.

Christians believe the concept of **original sin** can explain suffering (see p.6). God gave people **free will** — they **choose** to create suffering or good.
- St **Augustine** said suffering was the **price** people pay for **free will**.
- St **Irenaeus** thought people were created with **faults** because they had to **develop** into being **children of God** — so they needed **evil** and **suffering** to exist, else they'd have **no concept** of what's **right**.

Christians try to follow God's **example** of goodness — Psalms 119 asks for his **help** to do so. God can **punish** those who aren't good. He isn't only responsible for good — he creates **suffering** as a punishment.

> "I bring prosperity and create disaster" *Isaiah 45:7*

Muslims believe suffering can be a **test** from Allah. **Everything** is part of Allah's **plan** and there are good **reasons** for it, even if we can't see them. Evil gives people the chance to do **good** and help those in **need**. If we ourselves are **suffering**, Muslims believe we must bear it with **patience** and **faith**.

> "good tidings to the patient, who, when disaster strikes them, say, 'Indeed we belong to Allah'" *Qur'an 2:155-156*

 EXAM TIP

Revise thoroughly for the exam — else you'll suffer...

In the exam, read each question carefully. You've probably heard this a million times, but it's worth it — especially with complex topics such as these. You need to know exactly what's being asked.

Theme C — The Existence of God and Revelation

Revision Summary

A whole page of exam-style questions — just what you've been waiting for. They'll test whether you **remember** what you've learnt in the section, and get you used to what you'll be asked to do in the **exam**.

If there's anything you're not completely sure about, **go back** through the section and have another read of the relevant pages, then give the questions **another go**. There will be one question which has **extra marks** for **spelling**, **punctuation** and **grammar** — make sure you check your writing extra carefully for that one.

To get you warmed up, let's start with these 1 mark multiple choice questions.

1) Which of the following believe it's impossible to know for certain if God exists or not?
   a) Atheists   b) Humanists   c) Theologians   d) Agnostics

2) Which of the following is the theory developed by Darwin?
   a) Genesis   b) Big Bang theory   c) Theory of evolution   d) Design argument

3) Which of the following means all-powerful?
   a) Omnipotent   b) Omniscient   c) Infinite   d) Transcendent

4) Which of the following is not a type of revelation?
   a) Vision   b) God   c) Miracle   d) Scripture

You can get 2 marks for these, so make two short points in your answer.

5) Give two aspects of the First Cause argument.

6) Give two religious beliefs about special revelation.

7) Give two examples of how God's compassion might be shown through revelation.

8) Give two examples of people who have had visions.

Let's ramp it up with some 4 mark questions. Make two points and develop them further to get full marks. You need to write about the views of one or more religions.

9) Explain two contrasting religious beliefs about evolution.

10) Explain two similar religious beliefs about the scriptures as revelation.

11) Explain two similar religious beliefs about God's characteristics.

To make sure your longer answers are clear, make sure your answer is well-structured.

For this question, you must refer to the main religious tradition in the UK and at least one other religious viewpoint. This question is worth 4 marks.

12) Explain two contrasting beliefs about the revelation of God in nature.

For top marks in these 5 mark questions, you need to refer to religious texts.

13) Explain two religious beliefs about how creation proves the existence of God.

14) Explain two religious beliefs about miracles in the scriptures.

15) Explain two religious beliefs about how God can allow evil and suffering.

Finish on a high with this 12 mark question. It has an extra 3 marks available for spelling, punctuation and grammar. Before you begin, use the bullet points in the question to make a plan and structure your answer — you'll need to include all the things the bullet points ask for in your answer. Have a quick brainstorm of arguments for and against the statement.

16) 'God doesn't exist.'
    Evaluate this statement.
    Your answer should include the following:
    • arguments that support the statement
    • arguments that disagree with the statement
    • religious arguments
    • a conclusion

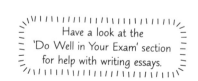

Have a look at the 'Do Well in Your Exam' section for help with writing essays.

General	**Peace and Conflict**

Peace is the absence of conflict and violence

- **Peace** means that everyone in the world lives in **harmony**, and there is **no conflict**.
- Many organisations, such as the **United Nations** (UN), work to find **peaceful solutions** to disputes and to **end all wars**, all over the world.
- Christianity and Islam both **encourage** believers to work towards **achieving peace** in the world.

Pacifism

Pacifists believe that **all** disputes should be settled **peacefully**.
- There were pacifists in Britain who **refused** to fight in the world wars.
  - Some of these '**conscientious objectors**' went to prison rather than go against their beliefs — they were **prisoners of conscience**.
  - They suffered **humiliation** in prison, and after they'd been released.
- There are different **degrees** of pacifism.
  - Some people are against violence **under any circumstances**.
  - However, others may **disagree** with violence, but understand that sometimes violence is the **least horrible** option.

> **pacifist**
> *someone who has strongly held beliefs that war and physical violence are wrong*

Violence happens for many different reasons

- CRIME — when criminal activity leads to violent acts, e.g. **assault** or **murder**.
- TERRORISM — when a person or group deliberately seeks to cause **fear** and inflict **suffering** on other people through **violence**, sometimes for **political** reasons.
- WAR — when two or more groups or countries **fight** one another. It's **usually** decided by **governments**.

> *The attack on the World Trade Center by the terrorist organisation al-Qaeda in New York in September 2001 was the worst terrorist attack in history.*

War and terrorism have caused many **deaths**. Lots of religious people believe that these acts are in **direct conflict** with the **sanctity of life** argument (see p.52).

- PROTEST — Most protests occur **peacefully**, but some protests can become **violent** if protesters with different views clash.

> **protest**
> *when groups of people join together to campaign for a cause they support*

Wars can have many causes

Most wars have causes that are a **combination** of lots of different factors:

RELIGION — this has been the cause of many **conflicts** in the past and the present (see p.65-67).

SELF-DEFENCE — wars started to **combat** a threat from another country or to **stop** them from attacking first, e.g. a **pre-emptive strike**.

TRIBALISM — this tends to trigger wars where a **group** of people fight for their own **independent** state.

HONOUR — wars fought to defend the **honour** and **dignity** of a country, or to **save face**.

GREED/ECONOMICS — **acts of aggression** (attacking without provocation) are **condemned** by the UN, so purely economic wars driven by greed (e.g. raids and invasions to gain territory or goods) are few and far between. Economic factors still have an impact though — **poverty** and **economic imbalances** can make wars **more likely**.

RETALIATION — a war might be started in **revenge** for something, e.g. **World War One** started after Franz Ferdinand, Archduke of Austria, was **assassinated**.

EXAM TIP

140 million people died in wars in the 20th century...

In this section, you have to know how Christians and Muslims view violence, weapons of mass destruction and pacifism, so make sure you know what's what.

Peace and Conflict

Some wars are seen as necessary and '**just**'. Others are sometimes seen as being fought for **God**.

Many people think there can be 'just' wars

Although most people see peace as being ideal, many recognise that sometimes a war has to be fought. Just War theory is a philosophical theory that explains the conditions for a war to be classed as necessary:

- There must be a good reason for the war, e.g. self-defence or to help innocent people under threat.
- All other options have been attempted to avoid war.
- It must be started by a proper authority — such as an elected government or president.
- A war must have a reasonable chance of success. Fighting an unwinnable war is considered a waste of lives.
- Any harm caused by fighting the war mustn't be as bad as the harm it's trying to prevent.

There are also two conditions for fighting a war justly. These are:

1 **Discrimination** — war should **discriminate** between **combatants** and **civilians**. It's not seen as 'just' to **deliberately** target civilians.

2 **Proportionality** — the military **advantage** gained by an attack must **outweigh** any **harm** to civilians.

Religious and non-religious people might turn to situation ethics (p.51) to decide if a war is 'just'. They'd look at all the factors, and choose what they think would most likely bring about peace.

People who fight in holy wars believe they're supported by God

A **holy war** is one where people believe that **God** is '**on their side**'. Wars are mentioned in both the **Old Testament** and the **Qur'an**.

It's worth noting that many religious people don't agree with war being fought over religion.

In the past, holy wars have been fought over **territory** or to **convert** people, e.g. the **crusades** in the 11th to 13th centuries. However, holy wars can be declared for different reasons, such as to **protect** a religion.

Religion has been a factor in **modern wars** too (though often not the only factor). E.g. although the **civil war** in Syria didn't start over religion, **Sunni** and **Shi'a** Muslims have fought on opposite sides.

Atheists and **humanists**, who don't believe in God, have **criticised** religion for causing conflict. Some atheists and humanists also identify as **pacifists**, and don't agree with conflict being used at all.

Christians believe people should be peaceful

Many of Jesus's teachings show that peace is the ultimate goal for all human beings

Isaiah 9:6 referred to the **Messiah** as the *"Prince of Peace"* (NIV).

For Christians, Jesus's command to *"Love your enemies"* (Luke 6:27 NIV) is very important in the way they live their lives. He said that people shouldn't follow the Old Testament teachings about retaliation:

> **"You have heard that it was said, 'Eye for eye, and tooth for tooth.' But I tell you... If anyone slaps you on the right cheek, turn to them the other cheek also."** *Matthew 5:38-39 NIV*

Christians believe Jesus was the Messiah and God wanted him to create peace on Earth.

This implies that Christians shouldn't meet violence with violence.

Even when Judas had betrayed him, Jesus didn't condone anyone being violent.

> **"All who draw the sword will die by the sword."** *Matthew 26:52 NIV*

This suggests that people who engage in conflict will die because of it.

Peace and Conflict

Many Christians follow Jesus's teachings and work for peace

Some Christians put Jesus's teachings into **action** and work to put an **end** to **violence** in the world.

> **Dorothy Day** was a Catholic **activist** who followed Jesus's **pacifist** teachings. She protested against the Spanish Civil War, WW2, violence and nuclear weapons in the USA (see p.68). She co-founded 'The Catholic Worker', a newspaper which was firmly **anti-war** and eventually evolved into a pacifist group of **campaigners**. She believed that Jesus's teachings mean Christians should be **pacifists**.

> Archbishop **Oscar Romero** worked for peace during turbulent times in 1970s **El Salvador**. He raised awareness of the **suffering** and **violence** people were being subjected to by the **military** and the **police**. He **helped** those affected by the cruelty, **fought** for their **rights** and **promoted peace** between opposing groups. He was killed for his beliefs in 1980.

> The Society of Friends (Quakers) is opposed to war under all circumstances.

Because of their belief in peace, Christians tend to use **passive resistance** against injustice — campaigning **without** violence:

> **Dr Martin Luther King** was a Baptist minister who dedicated his life to trying to change the way **black people** were treated in the USA. He organised **peaceful marches**, **rallies** and **boycotts**, and in 1965 blacks were given equal voting rights with whites.

> **Thomas Merton** was a Catholic monk and a famous **pacifist**. In the 1960s, his **writings** influenced many in the **civil rights movement** for racial equality and he was **against** the violence of the **Vietnam War**.

Most Christians **wouldn't** support violent protests, but some might think it's sometimes justified. For example, the quote below shows what Jesus did in protest when he saw that some people were **exploiting** the temple:

> **"[He] overturned the tables of the money changers and the benches of those selling doves"** *Matthew 21:12 NIV*

Some Christians recognise 'just' wars

- Although war goes **against** the teachings of **Jesus**, most Christian denominations **accept** that there can be such a thing as a **'just' war** (see p.65 for a reminder on the **Just War** theory).

- Some interpret this verse as meaning the government has the **right** to use **violence** to ensure peace:

> **"...if you do wrong, be afraid, for rulers do not bear the sword for no reason. They are God's servants, agents of wrath to bring punishment on the wrongdoer."** *Romans 13:4 NIV*

- The Catholic Church has **traditionally** accepted Just War theory:

> **"Legitimate defence can be not only a right but a grave duty for one who is responsible for the lives of others."** *Catechism of the Catholic Church 2265*

Holy wars are now rejected by nearly all Christians

- In the past, holy wars were fought to **convert** other people to Christianity. Jesus told his disciples:

> **"Do not suppose that I have come to bring peace to the earth. I did not come to bring peace, but a sword."** *Matthew 10:34 NIV*

> Many think Jesus actually meant that spreading the Christian message would cause divisions between believers and non-believers.

In the 11th, 12th and 13th centuries, Christians went on **crusades** to 'free' the Christian holy places in **Palestine**. The wars caused a lot of **devastation**.

- The **vast majority** of Christians **don't believe** in the idea of a holy war any more.
  - In fact, the Catholic Church is **reconsidering** its stance on war (see above) due to the **advanced weaponry** and **horrendous** impact of modern day war.
- Christians are strongly **against** the indiscriminate killing involved in **terrorism**.

EXAM TIP

I'll give you a peace of advice...

For 12 mark questions, both religious and non-religious opinions will help you get top marks.

Peace and Conflict

Islam teaches people to be peaceful

Islam promotes living a peaceful existence — the Qur'an teaches that people should be **kind** to others, even if they **don't** treat them well. Muslims believe Allah sees **everything** and will **judge** people.

> "And the servants of the Most Merciful are those who walk upon the earth easily, and when the ignorant address them [harshly], they say [words of] peace." *Qur'an 25:63*

> "If you should raise your hand against me to kill me - I shall not raise my hand against you to kill you. Indeed, I fear Allah, Lord of the worlds." *Qur'an 5:28*

Muslims believe they should play their part to bring about **peace**. They can do this in **three** ways:

 praying   campaigning   **3** working with people from **other religions** in the **community**

Muslim beliefs about war

The **majority** of Muslims **disagree** with **pacifism**, as war is sometimes **justified** in the Qur'an.

Some are **against** all war and violence as they believe **peaceful action** is always best, and is key to Islam.

> "Fight in the way of Allah those who fight you but do not transgress. Indeed. Allah does not like transgressors." *Qur'an 2:190*

Muslim beliefs about protests

Islam teaches people to protest against **injustice**, but **not** in **violent** ways. For example, the **Arab Spring** in 2011 saw many Muslims in countries such as Egypt demanding more **political power** for ordinary people. Many demonstrations were carried out **peacefully**, with a focus on **passive resistance**.

In Islam, a 'just' war is known as military jihad

War is an example of lesser jihad (see p.34). It must be fought only as a **last resort**. This passage from the Qur'an teaches that people can fight if necessary:

> "Allah will punish them by your hands and will disgrace them and give you victory over them..." *Qur'an 9:14*

Jihad involving **military action** is known as **Harb al-Maqadis** (holy war).

- It's a war considered to be justified by God to **protect** Muslims and their **religion**.
- Some believe that if they do **fight** for Allah, they'll be **rewarded** in the afterlife.

> "Those who believe fight in the cause of Allah." *Qur'an 4:76*

> "And he who fights in the cause of Allah and is killed or achieves victory — We will bestow upon him a great reward." *Qur'an 4:74*

Sunni and Shi'a Muslims both consider jihad a key part of their religion

In Shi'a Islam jihad is **formally** recorded as one of the **Ten Obligatory Acts** (p.31). In the past, **Twelver** Shi'a Muslims believed that jihad could **only** be declared when the **last Imam** came out of **hiding** (p.25), but jihad for **defensive** purposes was still **allowed**.

Military jihad has very strict **rules** — these are the **conditions** in Islam for a just war:

- It must bring about **freedom** from tyranny, restore **peace**, combat **oppression**, right **injustice** or be in **retaliation** to an attack.
- It must be in the name of Allah, according to his will, and declared by a **religious leader**.
- The hadith Muwatta Malik 21:10 also sets out some **conditions** for battle.
- In the past, jihad was used to spread Islam and gain more land. Now many Muslims believe jihad must not be used to colonise, suppress or impose Islam on non-believers.

> "Do not kill women or children or an aged, infirm person. Do not cut down fruit-bearing trees. Do not destroy an inhabited place." *Muwatta Malik 21:10*

- If the **opposition** wants to **end** the war, then Muslims must **accept** it:

> "And if they incline to peace, then incline to it [also]..." *Qur'an 8:61*

There are many similarities between the rules for military jihad and Just War theory (p.65).

! The term 'jihad' is sometimes used by Islamic **terrorists** to **justify** their acts of terror. However, nearly all Muslims are **strongly against** this — they don't consider the terrorists to be **real Muslims**.

Learn all the conditions for a just war in Islam...

Close the book, grab some paper and see how many Muslim beliefs on conflict you remember.

Christianity & Islam	# Weapons of Mass Destruction

Make sure you know what Christians and Muslims think about weapons of mass destruction.

Weapons of mass destruction cause a huge amount of damage

- **Weapons of mass destruction** (WMDs) can destroy large areas of land and kill lots of people all at once.
- They're **indiscriminate** — they harm soldiers and civilians alike.
- There are **several types** of WMDs, including:

nuclear   chemical   biological

Banned by international law — using them is a **war crime**.

There are many arguments for and against **possessing** nuclear weapons:

Views FOR possessing nuclear weapons	Views AGAINST

- Nuclear weapons serve as a **deterrent** to ensure peace — a country might **not** attack another if that country has nuclear weapons.
  - E.g. in the 20th century, several conflicts were settled or sidestepped because nuclear weapons posed too big a risk.
- Some have a **utilitarian** perspective — the best course of action is the one that brings about the best **balance** of positive and negative results.
  - E.g. the USA bombed Hiroshima and Nagasaki in Japan in WW2 as they thought that using nuclear weapons would save the most lives overall, and end the war faster.
- Nuclear weapons could be used by a country in order to **defend** itself if under attack.
	- Nuclear weapons are **costly**. **Funds** could be **better spent**, e.g. on healthcare.
	- **Widespread suffering** caused by nuclear weapons is unacceptable, and for religious people this completely goes against the belief in the **sanctity of life** (p.52).
	- The **indiscriminate nature** of nuclear weapons (they would kill innocent people) means that their use could **never** be classed as **just**.
	- Using nuclear weapons would **destroy** the environment and damage that which God trusted humans to take **care** of.

Many religious believers are against WMDs

Christian views

 Some Christians use Jesus's teachings about peace to argue against nuclear weapons. All Christian denominations are against using them.

 Christians might turn to Deuteronomy 20:

> **"When you lay siege to a city for a long time... do not destroy its trees by putting an axe to them, because you can eat their fruit."** *Deuteronomy 20:19 NIV*

This suggests that women and children should be spared, and unnecessary damage shouldn't be caused. The total destruction that WMDs would cause goes against this.

 Some think nuclear weapons help to keep the peace as countries are afraid of starting a nuclear war.

Muslim views

 Many Muslims are against WMDs as they don't follow the conditions of lesser jihad (see p.67) — innocent people would get hurt or killed.

> **"...whoever kills a soul... it is as if he had slain mankind entirely."** *Qur'an 5:32*

 Pakistan (a Muslim country) has nuclear weapons, but other Muslim countries have come out against possessing WMDs.

- Some **atheists** are in favour of WMDs to **deter** an opponent and to potentially **use** — they don't believe their **actions** will be **judged**.
- Others are strongly **anti-WMDs** as they believe people only live **one life** on Earth.
- **Humanists** have **opposed** the use of WMDs due to the **huge number** of people that would **suffer**.

 ## Make sure you know arguments for and against WMDs...

Explain two contrasting religious beliefs on nuclear weapons. [4]

Peacemaking

Finding peace and resolving conflicts is **important** to Christians and Muslims.

Justice, forgiveness *and* reconciliation *are key to peacemaking*

Justice

Justice is the idea of each person getting what they deserve, and maintaining what's right. Believers think that God is just — he treats and judges people fairly as he created everyone equally. Justice leads to a fairer society — if people feel they're treated equally, there's more chance of peace.

Forgiveness

Forgiveness is when a person stops feeling hurt by something another person has done to them. Another of God's characteristics is that he is merciful — he forgives people for the things they've done wrong. As God is merciful towards them, believers feel that they should forgive other people, and that forgiveness is the only way true peace can be achieved.

Reconciliation

Reconciliation is bringing people together that previously were in conflict to make peace.

Christians believe that God is fair and forgiving

Christians believe that justice is very important, since people are equal in the eyes of God. They have a duty to look after other people, and try to guide them to do what's right and repent of their sins.

> "...what does the Lord require of you? To act justly and to love mercy and to walk humbly with your God." *Micah 6:8 NIV*

They believe they should follow God's example and be just to others. The parable of the sheep and goats shows God treats people well if they've done the same to others.

Forgiveness is important to Christians (see p.75 for more about it). They believe they should seek God's forgiveness and forgive people who've hurt them.

> "Blessed are the merciful, for they will be shown mercy." *Matthew 5:7 NIV*

If they repent, and put their faith in God, God forgives people and they are reconciled with him. Christians believe the same sort of reconciliation is needed between people to create peace.

Muslims try to forgive and reconcile as Muhammad did

- Muslims believe strongly in justice and that they should treat all people fairly and equally. They consider maintaining justice to be part of their role as 'khalifah' — vice-regents of Allah's creation.
- Islam teaches that Allah and the Prophet Muhammad are forgiving (p.75).

> "And not equal are the good deed and the bad. Repel [evil] by that [deed] which is better; and thereupon the one whom between you and him is enmity [will become] as though he was a devoted friend." *Qur'an 41:34*

Muslims are encouraged to work to restore peace. They believe it's important to reconcile fractured relationships — this is something that the Prophet Muhammad did.

Learn it all — the examiner isn't as forgiving as God...

Draw a grid on a piece of paper. Down one side, write 'Christianity' and 'Islam'. Along the top, write 'Justice', 'Forgiveness' and 'Reconciliation'. Fill it in with what you've learned on this page.

Christianity & Islam	# Peacemaking

Many religious organisations work towards **peace** and help people in countries devastated by war.

Religious believers can work for peace directly and indirectly

Many religious believers feel they must act to create **peace** — see p.66 for some examples. People can work for peace either **directly** or **indirectly**.

> E.g. working with or for organisations which offer **relief** to war-torn areas.

> E.g. **donating** money to charitable causes, holding **protests** and **demonstrations** against conflicts, working to ensure that people have equal **human rights** (which could help to **avoid** conflict).

Christian charities work for peace and help victims of war

Many feel that it's important to **help people** caught up in **conflict zones** and to try to bring **peace** to the area. In the **Sermon on the Mount**, Jesus says:

> **"Blessed are the peacemakers, for they will be called children of God."** *Matthew 5:9 NIV*

Some religious **charities** exist to help achieve peace. They **campaign** for help for groups in conflict to **rebuild** their **relationship**, or assist people in **war-torn areas**. E.g.:

> **Christian Aid** is a charity that works to reduce poverty. It has urged governments to find a **compromise** in the Israel/Palestine conflict.

> **Pax Christi** is a Catholic organisation that works for peaceful conflict **resolution**. Read more about it in the last section of p.21.

> **Tearfund** helps people who are refugees from war-torn areas. They help people in the short term by giving them some food and somewhere to stay. However, they also help people to get back on their feet permanently by teaching them valuable skills they can use to support themselves.

Muslims can give money to support peacemaking

Muslims believe it's important to try to create a peaceful world. They believe that this is part of their role as khalifah.

Individuals can help to make the world more equal through zakah. Zakah could be donated to a number of different charities which are involved in peacemaking and supporting victims of war. E.g.:

> zakah
> *charitable giving where Muslims give 2.5% of their total savings (above a minimum amount) each year to the needy, no matter how rich or poor they are*

> **Muslim Peace Fellowship**
> A group of Muslims who want to promote peace, justice and non-violence.
> • It strives to do good through Islam — the group promotes peace through faith, and works to bring about changes that make society fair and compassionate to everyone.
> • They do this by raising awareness through events, prayer and working with other faiths.

> **Islamic Relief UK**
> A group inspired by their **faith** to try to help as many people as possible.
> • They help people affected by **war** — in **Syria** they've given people essentials such as **food** and **healthcare**.
> • They also help people in **neighbouring countries** who've **fled** their homes because of the **conflict**.

Peace, love, charity... and a nice revision task to end with...

How do religious believers work for a more peaceful world? Jot down as many ways as you can.

Revision Summary

That was a lot of information to take in there, so now test yourself to see how you got on. These questions are similar to the ones that you'll be answering in the exam, so you know what it'll be like on the day.

If there's anything you can't answer, go back through the section and have another go when you've re-read it. For some questions — you'll be told which ones — there are extra marks for spelling, punctuation and grammar, so check your writing carefully.

The exam will start with some nice 1 mark multiple choice questions.

1) Which of the following is the act of deliberately causing suffering and fear through violence?
   a) Passive resistance   b) Pacifism   c) Holy war   d) Terrorism

2) Which of the following is starting a war in revenge for something?
   a) Tribalism   b) Retaliation   c) Self-defence   d) Honour

3) Which of the following is the idea that everyone should get what they deserve?
   a) Justice   b) Peacemaking   c) Reconciliation   d) Forgiveness

4) Which of the following is the Muslim concept of charitable giving?
   a) Jihad   b) Utilitarianism   c) Zakah   d) Harb al-Maqadis

Moving up to 2 marks now, no biggy. 2 short points are all you need.

5) Give two religious beliefs about terrorism.

6) Give two examples of individuals who have worked for peace.

7) Give two religious beliefs about violent protest.

8) Give two religious beliefs about reconciliation.

4 marks now — make 2 points, but this time develop them for full marks.

9) Explain two similar religious beliefs about justice.

10) Explain two similar religious beliefs about forgiveness.

For these questions, you must refer to the main religious tradition in the UK and at least one other religious viewpoint. They're both worth 4 marks.

11) Explain two contrasting beliefs in Britain today about violence.

12) Explain two contrasting beliefs in Britain today about pacifism.

Make sure your writing is well structured and accurate in the longer questions — your points have to be clear to the examiner.

Next you'll face some 5 mark questions. You need to refer to religious texts in order to get all 5 marks.

13) Explain two religious beliefs about the importance of peace.

14) Explain two religious beliefs about just war.

15) Explain two religious beliefs about holy war.

16) Explain two religious beliefs about how peace can be achieved.

Hang on to your hat — it's the 12 mark question (plus 3 extra marks for SPaG). The question will come with a list of things to include, so use it when you start planning your answer. Write a list of arguments for and against the statement and make sure you've included them all.

17) 'It is justified for a country to possess nuclear weapons.'
    Evaluate this statement.
    Your answer should include the following:
    • religious arguments to support the statement
    • religious arguments that disagree with the statement
    • a conclusion
    You can also include non-religious points of view in your answer.

If you need advice on writing essays, have a look at the 'Do Well in Your Exam' section.

Christianity & Islam	# Religion and the Law

Most religions teach people to **follow** the **law**, but some people think that religious law should take **priority**.

People should do good and avoid evil

Christianity and Islam both teach people to live **good lives**.

This includes **following** religious **teachings**, e.g. by helping other people.

 The good things that people do will **please God/Allah**.

 People should **avoid** sin and evil, as their actions will be **judged** when they die.

In **CHRISTIANITY**, the **sheep** and **goats** parable (Matthew 25:31-46) says that everyone will be **judged** and **separated** into the **good** (the sheep) and the **bad** (the goats). Jesus said that **helping** another person is like helping **him**. If you **ignore** someone in need of help, it's like **ignoring him**.

Many Christians believe that **evil** is caused by humans **misusing** their **free will** — they believe that the **original sin** people are born with makes them **capable** of sin (see p.6). Some say **Satan** tempts people to sin.

> **"...whatever you did not do for one of the least of these, you did not do for me"**
> *Matthew 25:45 NIV*

ISLAM teaches that Allah is **merciful** and those who have done **good things** will be **rewarded**, but he will come down **harshly** on people who do **bad things**.

If people **intend** to do something **good**, that will **help** them on the **Day of Judgement**, but if they intend to do something **bad**, it **won't** count against them (see p.30).

Many Muslims believe that the **devil**, **Iblis**, tries to make humans turn to **evil**.

> **"He admits whom He wills into His mercy; but the wrongdoers - He has prepared for them a painful punishment."**
> *Qur'an 76:31*

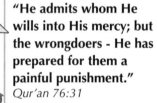

Law is essential to most societies

State
- The **laws of the state** define what's **right** and **wrong**, though this can **differ** from **religious ideas**.
- Most nations believe that the **rule of law** is the best way of **protecting** people in society. Without law there's the risk of **chaos**. With it, people know what they **can** and **cannot** do.
- In the UK, **laws** are rules made by Parliament and **enforced** by the courts.

Religious
- Christianity and Islam teach that **God** has commanded people to follow law. But some religious believers think that **religious law** is more important than the **laws of the land**.
- Where religious law and state law **disagree** some believers think it's better to commit a **crime** if it means they avoid committing a **sin** (see p.73).

For **CHRISTIANS**, there's a difference between a **sin** and a **crime**. A **sin** is when **religious** law is broken, i.e. when God's teaching is disobeyed. A **crime** is when the **state** laws are broken.

They have a **duty** to look after **other people**, and try to **guide** them to do what's right and **repent** of their sins.

MUSLIMS have a clear and detailed religious law (**shari'ah**), and this is often the **basis** for **state law** in Islamic countries. **Saudi Arabia**, for example, is run according to this religious law.

Shari'ah **councils** in **Britain** make rulings according to shari'ah law, but UK law takes **precedence**.

Justice is **important** to both Christianity and Islam.

justice
the idea of each person getting what they deserve (including punishing the guilty) and maintaining what's right (see p.69).

Learn about the law — and that's an order...

Write a short summary about what each religion teaches about good and evil.

Crime

Crime happens on a **daily** basis for many reasons, and it can take many **different forms**.

Many crimes break religious laws and teachings

There are many **different types** of crime, including **murder**, **theft** and **hate crimes**.

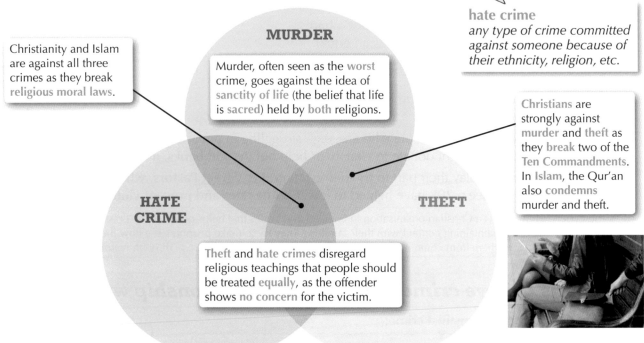

hate crime
any type of crime committed against someone because of their ethnicity, religion, etc.

Christianity and Islam are against all three crimes as they break **religious moral laws**.

MURDER

Murder, often seen as the **worst** crime, goes against the idea of **sanctity of life** (the belief that life is **sacred**) held by **both** religions.

HATE CRIME

THEFT

Christians are strongly against **murder** and **theft** as they **break** two of the **Ten Commandments**. In **Islam**, the Qur'an also **condemns** murder and theft.

Theft and **hate crimes** disregard religious teachings that people should be treated **equally**, as the offender shows **no concern** for the victim.

Crime is caused by lots of different factors

Most religious believers would agree that if someone does something **illegal**, they **deserve** to be **punished**. But the cause of crime **isn't** as simple as someone just being **bad** — there are many different **reasons** why a person might **commit** a **crime**:

POVERTY — People who are poor might turn to **crime** out of **desperation**. They might **steal food** or **money**, or earn **money** illegally, e.g. by selling stolen goods.

UPBRINGING — Some people might become criminals if they've had a **troubled childhood**, or if they've **grown up** around crime and it's become **normal** to them.

MENTAL ILLNESS — This can lead people to commit crimes because, e.g., they may not fully **understand** the **difference** between what's **legal** and **illegal**. Others may be easily **persuaded** into committing a crime.

ADDICTION — Being dependent on something such as **drugs** or **alcohol** can lead to people doing illegal things to **fund** their **addiction**.

GREED — Someone might **steal** or **earn** money **illegally** to get something they **want** but can't afford.

HATE — A person might do something illegal because someone else has **treated** them **badly**, or because they're driven by **prejudice**, e.g. racism.

OPPOSITION TO UNJUST LAW — A law might be **broken** as a **protest** if it's seen as unfair. In the 1950s and 60s many people, such as **Rosa Parks**, broke laws that treated black people **unfairly** in the **USA**.

Many feel that the **reason** behind the crime should be taken into **consideration**, and many religious people want to **help** the **individual** as well as tackle the **bigger issues** that cause crime. However, certain causes would be more likely to get **sympathy** than others, e.g. **poverty** would be seen as a more **acceptable** reason than **greed**. Many think that breaking a law that is **unfair** or that goes **against** religious law is **acceptable**.

Theme E — Religion, Crime and Punishment

Crime

Religions tend to **oppose** criminal actions, and many **religious organisations** work to put an **end** to them.

Christians work to prevent crimes

Christians are **strongly against** crime — they're told to **care** for others.

> **"Love your neighbour as yourself"** *Mark 12:31 NIV*

- Committing a crime such as **theft** or a **hate crime** doesn't treat the victim as an **equal**.
- **Murder** is seen as **destroying** something **created** by God.

> **"We must obey God rather than human beings!"** *Acts 5:29 NIV*

- Christians have **defied laws** to fight for what's **right**, e.g. Martin Luther King (see p.66). In this case, Christians may **support** breaking laws.
- Many Christians would **help** people who are, e.g., struggling in **poverty**, in order to tackle the **source** of crime. They might donate to **charity** or help out in **food banks**, among other things.
- **Christian groups** also play their part to try to **prevent** crime. **Street Pastors**, who help people out at night (see p.20), have helped to **lower** crime rates and **prevent violence**.

The **Prison Fellowship** is a Christian organisation in England and Wales that helps prisoners by **praying** for them and through **group activities** and maintaining **contact** with their **families**. They try to make prisoners see how they have **affected victims** of their crimes and **stop** them from **committing crime** again when they leave prison, e.g. through **restorative justice** (see p.75).

Muslims believe crime interrupts the relationship with Allah

Muslims are also **strongly against** crime:

- On **Yawn ad-Din** (the Day of Judgement — see p.30), those who've committed crimes might **not** be sent to **jannah**.
- A life of crime **doesn't** allow believers to **focus** on what really **matters** — their **faith** and connection with **Allah**.
- **Murder** is one of the **worst** crimes. **Theft** and **hate crimes** defy Islamic **teachings** about people being **equal**.

> **"Allah orders justice and good conduct and giving to relatives and forbids immorality and bad conduct and oppression."** *Qur'an 16:90*

> **"...whoever kills a soul... it is as if he had slain mankind entirely."** *Qur'an 5:32*

- Muslims hope that **key elements** of their religion help to **reduce** the likelihood of **crime**.

For example, **compulsory** charitable donations (**zakah** — see p.31) help to tackle poverty. Alcohol, drugs and gambling are **banned**, reducing the chance of **addiction**. Parents are taught to follow **teachings** in the Qur'an to give their child the best possible **upbringing**, which should **prevent** them from turning to crime. Some **mosques** offer help for families too.

- Islam teaches Muslims to **speak out** against **unjust laws** that go against Allah's teachings, so many would **understand** someone breaking an unjust law in **protest** against it.
- In **shari'ah courts**, the **circumstances** surrounding the crime are looked into **thoroughly**, so the defendant is punished **accordingly**.
- Some Muslims work to try to **reduce** crime by **helping prisoners** and **ex-offenders**:

The **Muslim Chaplains Association** offers **religious guidance** in **prisons** in the UK. It aims to **reform** prisoners and **stop** them from committing crimes after they are **released**, e.g. by helping them to **reintegrate** into society again. It also tries to keep ex-offenders **connected** to **chaplaincies** in their local **community** so they continue to receive **support** after prison.

Mosaic is a charity that pairs **young people** approaching the **end** of their prison sentence with a **mentor**. As they adjust to life outside of prison, the mentor will **help** them with things like finding a **job** and somewhere to **live** — with the aim that this should **prevent** them from returning to a life of **crime**.

There's lots to learn here, so have another read if you need...

'To prevent crime, we should tackle poverty.' Evaluate this statement.
Include religious arguments that support and disagree with the statement in your answer. [12]

Forgiveness	General, Christianity & Islam

Make sure you know different **religious views** about **forgiveness**.

Forgiveness can reunite people and prevent reoffending

Forgiveness means stopping being **angry** with someone who's done something **wrong**. Many religious people believe God is **merciful** towards people who **genuinely** seek his **mercy** and that they should **reflect** God's forgiving nature in their **own behaviour**.

Many believe forgiveness is important, so that...

...criminals can be **reconciled** with the **community**. If they leave prison **isolated** from others, with **no job** and **little prospects**, **reoffending** might seem like the **only option**. Forgiveness allows **both** victims and perpetrators to **move on**.

Forgiveness can be **shown** in many ways. **Lesser offences** no longer stay on people's **records permanently**, and there are **schemes** that give ex-offenders **skills** and a **job** when they're released.

Restorative justice can help people forgive

Restorative justice is where an offender might **meet** people who've **suffered** because of the crime they committed. Actually meeting the people they've hurt can help offenders to **realise** the **extent** of the **damage** they've done, try to **make up for** their actions and **discourage** them from **reoffending**. It helps the **victim** to work towards **forgiving** the offender.

 However, most religious people believe that **criminals** should still be **punished** for what they've done.

Christianity teaches that forgiveness comes from love

- Jesus taught that **God** is always ready to **forgive** and that Christians must **accept** that forgiveness, and forgive **others** in turn. The **Lord's Prayer** includes a verse about forgiveness (Matthew 6:12).

- Jesus told people to seek **reconciliation** in any disagreements **before** offering a **gift** to God at the temple:

> **"First go and be reconciled to them; then come and offer your gift."** *Matthew 5:24 NIV*

- He also taught people to forgive *"not seven times, but seventy-seven times"* (Matthew 18:22 NIV).

- Forgiveness is closely related to **repentance**. Christians believe that God's forgiveness can only come when they **repent** of their sins (i.e. say sorry, and turn their backs on them).

Islam teaches that Allah is forgiving

- Muslims can seek **retribution** (see p.76) for injuries, but they're encouraged to **forgive** instead. Whenever the **Qur'an** describes **punishment**, it talks about **forgiveness** too.

- Muslims believe that they must be **merciful** so that **Allah** will do the **same** to them on **Yawm ad-Din** (the Day of Judgement).

- They believe that wrongdoing should be forgiven if the offender is **sorry** and tries to **make amends**.

> **"But if you pardon and overlook and forgive - then indeed, Allah is Forgiving and Merciful."** *Qur'an 64:14*

The **Prophet Muhammad** was forgiving, as told in the Hadith — Muslims believe in **following** his **example**.

 But some crimes are seen as so awful that forgiveness isn't an option, e.g. shirk (see p.26).

 ## *Forgive and forget (but not your revision)...*

Explain two religious beliefs about forgiveness. You should include sacred text references. [5]

Theme E — Religion, Crime and Punishment

General, Christianity & Islam	# Punishment

Punishment can be used to 'get back' at someone for committing a crime, or to prevent crime in the future.

Punishment can have various aims

Punishment is **needed** in society so that people **follow** the **law**. Criminals should face the **consequences** for their actions and victims should get **justice**. Punishment has many **purposes**:

Retribution

Some people think of punishment as a way of taking **revenge** on a criminal, of making them '**pay**' for what they've done. Critics of this way of thinking argue that revenge **doesn't put right** the wrong — that it's better to look for a more **constructive** solution.

Protection

If a criminal is considered **dangerous**, then their punishment should **protect** the rest of **society**, e.g. imprisonment. Not many people would disagree with this, but some would argue that you protect society best by **reforming** offenders.

Reformation

Punishment should aim to **change** criminals so they won't offend again — the idea being that nobody is inherently **bad**. Many religious people feel this allows offenders to **repent** and seek **forgiveness** from God for their actions. Programmes to reform criminals include **counselling** and giving them **work** in the community.

Deterrence

This is the idea that if a punishment is sufficiently **bad** in some way (e.g. expensive, embarrassing, restricting, painful) it will **put people off** committing the crime because they understand the **consequences**. Critics argue that people don't **stop to think** about punishment before they commit a crime, especially if they've taken drugs or alcohol, so deterrence **doesn't work**.

There are various Christian views on the aims of punishment

- Christians think that criminals should be punished for what they've done in a just way.

 Some think punishment should be *"eye for eye"* (Leviticus 24:20 NIV), so focus on **retribution**.

 Others believe they should *"turn... the other cheek"* (Matthew 5:39 NIV), and so look more towards **reformation**.

- Being **merciful** is important in Christianity, and Christians believe **reformation** is **important**.

> "...if someone is caught in a sin, you who live by the Spirit should restore that person gently."
> *Galatians 6:1 NIV*

- Christians also value **deterrence** and **protection** — these help make communities **less dangerous**.

- Jesus told people to look at their **own behaviour** before **criticising** others. In John 8, a woman who was accused of **adultery** was **saved** by Jesus when he said:

> **"Let any one of you who is without sin be the first to throw a stone at her."** *John 8:7 NIV*

No-one did, and it reminds Christians that everyone sins.

Islamic punishments held publicly deter people

> "Allah wants to make clear to you [the lawful from the unlawful] and guide you to the [good] practices of those before you and to accept your repentance."
> *Qur'an 4:26*

- Many Muslims believe in **reformation**, and punishment should give criminals the opportunity to **see** the error of their ways.

- The Qur'an mentions punishments such as **whipping** that are carried out **publicly** — the aim of this is to **deter** the criminal, but some believe this form of punishment can **reform** offenders too, and offers **retribution**. See p.77 for how this is applied **today**.

- The Qur'an also says that the **punishment** should **fit** the **crime**: *"...an eye for an eye..."* (Qur'an 5:45). But Qur'an 2:178 explains that the offender can sometimes **compensate** the victim **financially**.

Theme E — Religion, Crime and Punishment

Punishment

Punishments **vary** according to the crime, and religious believers hold **different views** on these punishments.

There are many different types of punishment

Depending on the **severity** of the **crime** committed, criminals can be given **various sentences**, including **prison**, **community service** and (in countries where it's legal) **corporal punishment**.

 Some religious people believe community service allows the offender to **repay** their **debt** to society yet still lead a **normal life**, which should help to **ensure** they don't **reoffend**. Some Muslims believe it's **too easy** and **doesn't stop** reoffending.

Corporal punishment is **not** used in **Europe**, but it is used **elsewhere** in the world.

Some people might argue that corporal punishment and the **suffering** it causes would put people off **reoffending**. Some think that life in **prison** should be **difficult** in order to make offenders **think twice** about **crime**. They might also think that treating prisoners **harshly** can be **more effective** in **reforming** them.

Prisoners have **human rights** — many argue corporal punishment goes **against** this and promotes **violence**.

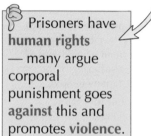 **corporal punishment** *when a criminal is punished through physical pain delivered by, e.g., beating or flogging them.*

Religions have some **conflicting views** on whether or not corporal punishment should be used:

Views FOR corporal punishment	Views AGAINST corporal punishment
CHRISTIANITY • There are **examples** in the **Bible** of corporal punishment being used on criminals (Deuteronomy 25:2), so it's **acceptable** in some situations. • The Bible can be seen to suggest that **disciplining** children through **corporal punishment** is **allowed**: *"Whoever spares the rod hates their children." Proverbs 13:24 NIV*	• Christians believe that prisoners have the **right** to be treated **fairly** — many want **better conditions** in prison and visit **offenders** in prison. *"Speak up and judge fairly; defend the rights of the poor and needy." Proverbs 31:9 NIV* • The **majority** of Christians are **strongly against** corporal punishment — Jesus was against violence: *"all who draw the sword will die by the sword." Matthew 26:52 NIV* • Many **disagree** with corporal punishment as it goes against the idea of Christian **compassion**.
ISLAM • Under **shari'ah law**, corporal punishment is **permissible** for certain crimes, such as drinking **alcohol** and **stealing**: *"[As for] the thief... amputate their hands in recompense for what they committed as a deterrent [punishment] from Allah." Qur'an 5:38*	• The Qur'an teaches that **prisoners** should be treated **fairly**: *"And they give food in spite of love for it to the needy, the orphan, and the captive" Qur'an 76:8* • There are **rigorous rules** about the **evidence** needed before using corporal punishment, and many Muslim countries **don't** actually **use** it. Some Muslims believe corporal punishments are **too severe**, and don't respect the offender's **human rights**.

 ## Don't do the crime if you can't do the time...
You must learn views from Christianity and Islam on corporal punishment.

General, Christianity & Islam

The Death Penalty

The death penalty is **killing** someone as punishment for a crime — it's also called **capital punishment**.

The death penalty isn't used much nowadays

- Capital punishment has been **abolished** in many countries, including most of Europe and South America. Elsewhere, it only tends to be used for **very serious** crimes, e.g. **murder**, **espionage** (spying) and **treason**.

- **Religious** and **non-religious** people might make some of these **arguments** for and against the death penalty:

FOR the death penalty

- The risk of death might act as a **better deterrent** to violent criminals than a prison sentence.

- If you execute a murderer, it's **impossible** for them to **kill again**. Imprisoned murderers have been known to **order** killings from jail, or to **reoffend** when released on parole. In cases like these, the **suffering** of the criminal could potentially **protect** many people.

- **Utilitarianism** (or the **principle of utility**) is the idea that the **best** course of action creates the best **balance** of **good** and **bad** results, e.g. it could be used to argue that killing criminals, although bad for them, would be good for the **majority** of society.

AGAINST the death penalty

- Killing as punishment is **just as bad** as murder — many **religious people** and **Humanists** are against **any** form of killing.

- It doesn't give the offender the chance to **reform**.

- There have been cases where someone has been proved **innocent after** having been executed.

- Life is **special** and should be **preserved** — many religious people believe in the **sanctity of life**.

- Many religious believers think **God alone** can decide when to **end** someone's **life**.

✝ **Christians** might be against the death penalty because the **Ten Commandments** forbid killing.

BUT... ...some people might use **situation ethics** to decide on a **case-by-case** basis if the death penalty should be applied. This could lead to people being **for** the death penalty in **some** cases, but **against** it in **others**, depending on, e.g., the **severity** of the crime and the **background** to the case.

Christians have mixed views on capital punishment

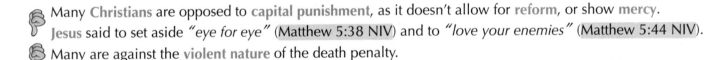

Many **Christians** are opposed to **capital punishment**, as it doesn't allow for **reform**, or show **mercy**. Jesus said to set aside *"eye for eye"* (Matthew 5:38 NIV) and to *"love your enemies"* (Matthew 5:44 NIV).

Many are against the **violent nature** of the death penalty.

However, some Christians in the **United States** (where capital punishment is **legal**) believe that the death penalty is a **good** thing. They say it **protects** the innocent. They might refer to **biblical texts** such as:

> **"Anyone who strikes a person with a fatal blow is to be put to death."** *Exodus 21:12 NIV*

> **"Whoever sheds human blood, by humans shall their blood be shed."** *Genesis 9:6 NIV*

Islamic law allows the death penalty

Some Muslims believe that **Allah**, not humans, should decide when **life ends** — they **don't** agree with capital punishment.

The Qur'an outlines crimes punishable by **death**, but **encourages** victims' families to take **compensation**.

Muhammad said that death could be a punishment in **three** cases:

> **"the married adulterer, a life for life, and the deserter of his Din (Islam)"** *Sahih Muslim 16:4152*

This is reflected in **shari'ah law**.

EXAM TIP

Learn contrasting views on the death penalty for the exam...

You must know views from Christianity and Islam about the death penalty.

Revision Summary

And that wraps up another section — time to see how you got on. The **questions** below are the **same style** as the questions you'll be answering in the **actual exam**.

If there's anything you can't answer, **go back** through the section and have **another go** when you've **re-read it**. For some questions — you'll be told which ones — there are **extra marks** for **spelling**, **punctuation** and **grammar**, so check your writing carefully.

Jumping right in with some 1 mark multiple choice questions.

1) Which of the following is the Islamic law followed in some countries? □
   a) Hadith   b) Shari'ah   c) Zakah   d) Yawm ad-Din

2) Which of the following is where an offender might meet their victim? □
   a) Corporal punishment   b) Prison   c) Community service   d) Restorative justice

3) Which of the following is the idea that punishment should try to change the criminal for the better? □
   a) Protection   b) Reformation   c) Retribution   d) Deterrence

4) Which of the following is the idea that the best action is the one with the best balance of good and bad? □
   a) Sanctity of life   b) Situation ethics   c) Utilitarianism   d) Compensation

For these 2 mark questions, keep it short and snappy with 2 brief points.

5) Give two religious beliefs about the laws of the state. □
6) Give two examples of causes of crime. □
7) Give two ways that religious people can help to prevent crime. □
8) Give two arguments against capital punishment. □

It's a similar idea with these 4 mark questions, but this time develop your points a bit more.

9) Explain two similar religious beliefs about breaking unjust laws. □
10) Explain two similar religious beliefs about preventing crime. □
11) Explain two similar religious beliefs about prison as a form of punishment. □

Make sure your longer answers are well organised and clearly written so the examiner can easily see your points.

For this question, you must refer to the main religious tradition in the UK and at least one other religious viewpoint. This is worth 4 marks.

12) Explain two contrasting religious beliefs about corporal punishment. □

And the questions continue — this time for 5 marks. Refer to sacred texts for full marks.

13) Explain two religious beliefs about why people should live good lives. □
14) Explain two religious beliefs about murder. □
15) Explain two religious beliefs about retribution as an aim of punishment. □
16) Explain two religious beliefs about reformation as an aim of punishment. □

Saving the best for last — the 12 mark question with 3 additional marks for SPaG. The question will have a list of information that you need to include, so use it to make a plan. Jot down arguments for and against the statement so you don't forget any when you actually start writing your answer.

17) 'The death penalty is never a suitable punishment.'
    Evaluate this statement.
    Your answer should include the following:
    • religious arguments that support the statement
    • religious arguments that disagree with the statement
    • a conclusion
    You can also include non-religious points of view in your answer. □

Head over to the 'Do Well in Your Exam' section for help with writing essays.

Theme E — Religion, Crime and Punishment

Attitudes to Equality

You need to be aware of **different views** in **British society** for this **whole section**. You need to be able to give **Christian** views on the **status** of **women** in **religion**, as well as views on this from **one** other **religious tradition**.

Prejudice and discrimination prevent equality

Difference in wealth is another form of inequality — see p.86-88.

- **Prejudice** relates to the **views** a person holds — **discrimination** happens when they **act** on those views:

prejudice
judging something or someone for no good reason, or without full knowledge of a situation.

discrimination
treating someone unjustly or differently, often because of prejudice

- **Prejudice** comes in **different forms**, e.g.:

sexism
the belief one gender is inferior to the other

racism
prejudice against people of other races

homophobia
prejudice against people who are homosexual

- The **Equality Act 2010** says it's **illegal** to **discriminate** on the grounds of '**protected characteristics**', which include race, gender, age and sexual orientation. The Act aims to ensure everyone is treated **equally**.

- **Positive discrimination** may be used when assessing **job applications** made by people from groups that are often discriminated against — it's only legal if they're **as well qualified** as the other applicants.

positive discrimination
when someone in a group that often suffers discrimination is given an advantage.

Christianity teaches equality

"Do to others what you would have them do to you" is a fundamental part of Christian teaching, often called the 'Golden Rule'. Many Christians think everyone was created equal, so they try to avoid discrimination.

"Love your neighbour as yourself" *Mark 12:31 NIV*
Jesus said that this is the second most important commandment, after loving God.

"A new command I give you: love one another" *John 13:34 NIV*
i.e. don't mistreat others.

"...discrimination ... on the grounds of sex, race, colour, social conditions, language, or religion must be ... eradicated as incompatible with God's design" *Catechism of the Catholic Church 1935*

The **Good Samaritan** parable is an important teaching on **prejudice**. Two **holy** men **ignore** a man who's been **beaten** and **robbed**. He's then **helped** by a **Samaritan**, a group who were **despised** at the time. The story shows how **prejudices** can be **wrong**.

Islam says people are created equal, but not identical

- Islam teaches that all people were created by Allah, and were created equal (although not the same). He intended humanity to be created with differences. But this just means we're all individuals.

- Muslims all over the world are united by the ummah. The ummah consists of all Muslims, regardless of nationality, tradition (i.e. Sunni or Shi'a) and so on. This helps promote racial and social harmony, as in theory no one's excluded or discriminated against.

ummah
the community of Islam

- People on hajj all wear simple white clothes, showing everyone's equal — race, gender etc. don't matter.

- Sahih al-Bukhari 56:681 says everyone should be treated the same way, regardless of who they are.

Attitudes to Equality

Traditionally, religions have supported different gender roles

Christian attitudes to gender equality have shifted

For more on this, see p.45.

Traditionally...

Christians believed **women's roles** were to look after the **home** and **children**, while **men** earned **money** and **led** the family.

Now...

Some **still** believe this, but **most** now think **both** genders can do **either role**.

Women had **less authority** in **religion** — there were no female **church leaders** for centuries.

There are now female ministers in most **Protestant** denominations, though not **Catholic** or **Orthodox** ones.

Men and women have different roles within Islam

The **Qur'an** makes it **clear** that men and women are **equal** when it comes to their **religious obligations**, e.g. prayer, fasting, hajj and charity — have a look at Qur'an 33:35 on p.45, which also has more information on **gender equality**.

All that counts is how good a **Muslim** they are, not their **gender**:

> "O mankind, indeed We have created you from male and female and made you peoples and tribes that you may know one another. Indeed, the most noble of you in the sight of Allah is the most righteous of you." *Qur'an 49:13*

Prayer

- Women don't **have** to attend mosque for **prayer**, but it is **permitted**. If women do go to the mosque, they must pray in a **separate** group — behind (or otherwise out of sight of) the men. This is because it's thought it might be distracting for both genders to pray in a mixed group.
- Women can't lead prayers in **mixed groups**, but they can lead prayers being said by groups of **women**.
- There is a growing movement working for women to have a more **prominent role** in Islam. Several women have led **mixed-gender** prayers across the world. Their actions have been **condemned** by some Muslims as not following the teachings of Islam. There are plans for a **mosque** run by women in Bradford.

Clothing

- Some say it's **part of Islam** for Muslim women to wear **modest clothing**.

> "...tell the believing women ... to wrap [a portion of] their headcovers over their chests and not expose their adornment." *Qur'an 24:31*

- Others argue it doesn't say they have to cover up **completely** and that their **faith** and **piety** are more **important** than clothing.

> "the clothing of righteousness — that is best." *Qur'an 7:26*

EXAM QUESTION

So, now you know these pages off by heart and backwards...

...try this exam question. If you don't feel you know the topic well enough, read the pages again.
'Men and women should have the same roles within religion.' Evaluate this statement, making sure you refer to religious views which support and disagree with it, and give a conclusion. [12]

Attitudes to Equality

Christian and Muslim teachings oppose racism

CHRISTIANITY

- Christianity teaches that racism is unacceptable, and God made everyone equal.

> "you are all one in Christ Jesus" Galatians 3:28 NIV

> "From one man he made all the nations" Acts 17:26 NIV

- This means many Christians believe it's their duty to fight racism. This can be done by an individual, e.g. by welcoming someone of another ethnicity to the community, or at an institutional level, e.g. a church asking its members to treat everyone equally. The Church of England recommends that people make "neighbours out of strangers" in its report Faithful Cities.

- Racial equality can be difficult to achieve. The Church of England has been criticised for not having enough ethnic minority people among its clergy — it's now making efforts to increase diversity.

> Desmond Tutu is an Anglican archbishop who fought against apartheid in South Africa, in which the white minority population oppressed everyone else. After apartheid ended, he led the Truth and Reconciliation Commission, which investigated the crimes of the apartheid era and focused on the unity of all people.

ISLAM

The final sermon of Muhammad is clear that no race is superior to another:

> "...you are all descended from Adam and none is higher than the other except in obedience to Allah. No Arab is superior to a non-Arab. Between Muslims there are no races and no tribes."
> Final sermon of Muhammad

The only important thing is whether someone's a good Muslim or not.

> Malcolm X was a prominent figure in the struggle for civil rights for African Americans in the US. He initially advocated black supremacy and separatism, but later supported interethnic dialogue. He inspired many with his campaigning for human rights.

Homosexuality is controversial in both Christianity and Islam

	Views SUPPORTING homosexuality	Views AGAINST homosexuality
CHRISTIANITY	• Many Christians focus on loving their neighbour and therefore accept homosexuality. • Many individual members of the Church of England and the Catholic Church disagree with their Churches' stances on homosexuality.	• Homosexuality is a sin, and is forbidden by Bible teachings such as 1 Corinthians 6:9-10. • Church of England bishops issued a report in 2017 saying they wouldn't change the Church's definition of marriage as being between one man and one woman (Canon B30). • The Catechism of the Catholic Church 2357 says homosexual acts are "contrary to the natural law".
ISLAM	• As Allah created all people, homosexuality is part of his creation. • Muslims often speak against homophobia, as Muslims should be tolerant towards others. • Some Muslim organisations, such as Imaan, support homosexual Muslims and campaign for their rights.	• Many Muslims believe that the Qur'an forbids homosexuality, as in the quotation below (which is addressed to men): "you approach men with desire, instead of women ... you are a transgressing people" Qur'an 7:81 • This means they're against the legalisation of same-sex marriage.

 • Some Muslim organisations state that they are against homosexual acts but believe homosexual people should be respected.

Human Rights

Human rights are **moral**, **legal** and **political** rights that should give people **freedom** and **protection** worldwide.

The United Nations defined human rights

In 1948, the United Nations (UN) published the Universal Declaration of Human Rights. This **stated** how things **should** be, but meant **nothing** in a court of law. So in 1953, the Council of Europe brought into effect the European Convention on Human Rights.

The Universal Declaration of Human Rights

• Its aim was to lay down minimum **rights** for **every person**, in **every country**.
 • It states that all human beings are born **free** and **equal** in dignity and rights.
 • It also lists specific rights, e.g.:
   • the right to **life**
   • freedom from **slavery**
   • freedom from **imprisonment** or **exile** without **good reason**
   • freedom of **opinion** and **expression**
   • the right to have an **education** and to seek **work**

European Convention on Human Rights
• This is a **similar** list of rights to the UN declaration.   • It's enforced by the European **Court** of Human Rights (ECHR).   • These rights became part of the UK's **domestic law** in 1998, with the **Human Rights Act**.

The European Court of Human Rights. (I think.)

Most religious believers agree that all human beings should be treated **fairly** and with **respect**. This is based on a belief in **human dignity** — all human life is **valuable**, because people are created in the **image of God** — and a belief in **justice**, the idea that everyone should be treated **fairly**. Everyone should be **free** to **think** and to **choose** how to act (though hopefully they'll live a good **moral** life).

Many Christians support human rights

The **Catholic Church** highlights the role of the **individual** as well as the **state** in **protecting** human rights. It says human rights aren't just defined by **states** putting them into **law**:

> **"Every member of the community has a duty ... in order that the rights of others can be satisfied and their freedoms respected."** *The Common Good and the Catholic Church's Social Teaching: 37*

Christians may find their views **contradict** others' ideas about rights. E.g. many think **women** should have the right to **abortion**, but some Christians **disagree**, believing the **foetus's** right to **life** is more **important**.

> **"You ... were called to be free. But do not use your freedom to indulge the flesh; rather, serve one another humbly in love."** *Galatians 5:13 NIV*

The Qur'an says justice is very important

Most Muslims are supportive of human rights. The **Qur'an** frequently emphasises the **importance** of **justice**:

> **"O you who have believed, be persistently standing firm for Allah, witnesses in justice ... Be just; that is nearer to righteousness."** *Qur'an 5:8*

> **"Indeed, Allah orders justice and good conduct and giving to relatives and forbids immorality and bad conduct and oppression. He admonishes you that perhaps you will be reminded."** *Qur'an 16:90*

Some Muslims argue that **Islamic law** sometimes **undermines** Muslim **women's** rights, e.g. they don't have **equal rights** in **divorce** to men (see p.41).

REVISION TASK

The right to drink tea is an important part of British law...

...just kidding. Quite a good idea though. Anyway, back to business — shut the book and have a go at writing down as many of the human rights on the page as you can remember.

Freedom of Belief

You need to be able to give **contrasting** religious views on this **topic**.

The UK is a diverse, multi-faith society

- **Freedom of religion** and **belief** is a **legal** right in the UK — it gives the freedom to follow **any** or **no** religion.
- People are protected from being **discriminated** against because of their **beliefs**.
  The **beliefs** they hold as part of their religion are **protected**, e.g. religions can choose **not** to hold **same-sex marriages** in their **places of worship** if it doesn't fit with their **beliefs**.

About half of the population say they have no religious belief.

Freedom of belief is sometimes a tricky area though...

- Some people feel there isn't **enough recognition** of those who **don't** hold religious beliefs, e.g. in **religious studies** in **schools**.
- There can be a fine line between **educating** people about a **faith** and **influencing** them too much. Some people think, e.g.:

> **Religious charities** have too much influence.

> The charities aren't trying to **convert** people, just **help** them.

- Some people, including religious believers, object to the **Church of England** being the **state church**, e.g.:

> 26 **bishops** are peers in the **House of Lords**, which is **unfair** now that the country is more religiously **diverse** and many people **don't have** a religion at all.

> The UK is a **Christian** country so it's acceptable — it's part of the **culture**.

- A religious person saying homosexuality is **sinful** clashes with homosexual people's **right** not to be **discriminated** against and could be seen as **hate speech** (a **crime**), but **stopping** people from expressing their views **undermines** their **freedom of belief**.

- Most religious believers happily live alongside others in the UK and enjoy the **different perspectives** it gives them. The **Inter Faith Network for the UK** promotes mutual **understanding** and **combats prejudice**.
- Living in a multi-faith society can make it **harder** for some believers to **practise** their **faith** — e.g. some **Christian** festivals are UK **bank holidays** while other faiths' festivals **aren't**, making it **harder** to **celebrate**.

Many Christians think people can follow any faith

- Though many Christians think Christianity's the **true** religion, they think people have the **right** to practise **any faith**.
- Some Christians think the **only way** to reach heaven is by being Christian, so they try to **convert** people.

> **"[It's] an inalienable requirement of the dignity of man."** *Catechism of the Catholic Church 1747*

The Qur'an says people are free to choose their religion

Muslims believe that Islam is the only **true** faith — but they also believe that all **righteous** people will be favoured by Allah. Most Muslims **don't** try to **convert** others to Islam.

> **"There shall be no compulsion in [acceptance of] the religion."** *Qur'an 2:256*

APOSTASY

However, Muslims' freedom of belief is often **restricted** by the **common** belief that converting to **another** religion **from** Islam or becoming an **atheist** is **unacceptable** in Islam — it's known as **apostasy**.

- Some **hadiths** say it deserves the **death penalty**.
- Some Muslims **disagree**, as the Qur'an leaves **judgement** up to **Allah**.
- It can be **hard** for ex-Muslims — they're often **cut off** from their family.

> **"whoever desires other than Islam ... he, in the Hereafter, will be among the losers"** *Qur'an 3:85*

Muslims call **Muslims**, **Christians** and **Jews** 'people of the book', as they're linked by a **shared** religious **heritage**. They all believe in **prophets** such as Ibrahim (Abraham) and many Muslims believe the **Torah** and **New Testament** contain **important messages**.

> **"our God and your God is one"** *Qur'an 29:46*

I can't do GCSEs, exams are against my religion...

...sorry, that won't wash. Try this exam-style question instead.

Explain two contrasting religious beliefs about freedom of belief. [5]

Theme F — Religion, Human Rights and Social Justice

Social Justice

Social justice is the idea that everyone should have equal rights and opportunities.

Social justice *is the idea that* everyone should be treated *fairly*

Social justice is putting into practice the principles of human rights.

> **Working for social justice includes:**
> - Trying to ensure different groups of people aren't discriminated against or more disadvantaged than others. This includes discrimination on the grounds of race, gender, religion, social class, poverty, age or disability.
> - Trying to redistribute wealth so everyone can afford to live comfortably. Some members of society are very wealthy while others struggle to meet their basic needs for food, shelter, warmth, etc.

- Social justice efforts often focus on wealth, as a lack of it can deprive people of other opportunities and rights. Higher taxes for people on high incomes and free healthcare and education are ways to help.
- Many people try to work for social justice. It's an important part of Christianity and Islam.

Christianity *teaches that people should* help those in need

Christians follow Jesus's teaching to *"Love your neighbour as yourself"* Mark 12:31 NIV.
The parable of the sheep and goats is often used to teach about social justice — see p.22 for more.

> Jesus was known for helping poor people and for healing the sick. In Luke 16:19-31, he teaches that people who don't help others when they're able to will be punished — the story is about a rich man who repeatedly ignores a poor man, and ends up in hell for not helping him. Jesus healed a man with leprosy by touching him, at a time when lepers were outcasts from society. Christians should therefore follow Jesus's example — by helping those who need it, they can express God's love.

The Catholic Church emphasises the importance of human dignity in social justice.

> "[people should be allowed] to obtain what is their due, according to their nature and their vocation" *Catechism 1928*

> This means people should be given opportunities to make the most of their lives and their abilities. Catechism 1928 also says social justice is better for everyone — it's for *"the common good"*.

Islam *encourages helping others*

- Muslims should work for social justice as part of their faith:

> "[the righteous] give food in spite of love for it to the needy, the orphan, and the captive, [Saying] ... We wish not from you reward or gratitude." *Qur'an 76:8-9*

> This means people should give help without expecting anything in return.

- Zakah, charitable giving to redistribute wealth, is central to Islam — it's one of the five pillars (see p.31).

> "[those who] give zakah ... will be the successful" *Qur'an 7:156-157*

- It promises that those who have wealth to spare and give it away will be rewarded.

> "Those who spend their wealth [in Allah's way] ... — they will have their reward with their Lord." *Qur'an 2:274*

Basically, everyone should help people who need it...

There are a few different teachings on this page, so as a fun test (or maybe just a test...), write down as many as you can remember without looking at the page. Don't forget to give the source.

Theme F — Religion, Human Rights and Social Justice

Wealth and Poverty

How **wealth** is **used**, and how it's **distributed** among people, is a **big issue** today. For the **exam**, you need to be able to give **Christian** opinions on the **uses of wealth**, as well as views from **one other religious** tradition.

Wealth inequality is a big problem today

The **gap** between the **poorest** and **richest** people is **huge**, and **growing**. In 2017, **Oxfam** estimated that the richest **8** people in the world had **more wealth** than the poorest **half** of the world (**3.6 billion** people).

> **poverty**
> *not having enough resources (money, etc.) to meet your basic needs, e.g. food or heating*

Causes of poverty include...

In the UK

- low wages
- high costs (e.g. renting a house or paying for childcare)
- a lack of skills so people can't get better-paid jobs
- unemployment

> In the UK, the poorest 50% of people own 8.7% of wealth, while the richest 10% own 45%.

- **Fair pay** is an issue. Many in **poverty** have **low-paid** jobs, so they work **long hours** to try to earn enough to live on. In some **areas**, **well-paid** jobs **aren't** available. **Part-time** work's often low-paid.
- By law, people have to be paid the National Minimum Wage, but many people think it **isn't** enough. Over-25s must be paid the National Living Wage, which is a bit **higher** than the minimum wage. However, many say it still isn't **enough** to **live on** — it's not a **true** living wage.
- **Businesses** are often **reluctant** to pay people **more** as it's **expensive** for them to do so — some try to **avoid** paying even the minimum wage. Some say **increasing** wages will mean they **can't afford** to **pay** people so they would have to **cut** the number of jobs, which wouldn't help.

Worldwide

- war
- rapid population growth
- natural disasters
- exploitation

> The **Fairtrade Foundation** works to ensure people in **developing countries** are paid a **fair price** for the products they **sell** and that they have **decent working conditions**.

Finding a solution is difficult

- Helping to relieve poverty caused by **disasters** (e.g. **war**) often needs **emergency relief** during the **disaster** and **long-term** help afterwards, e.g. rebuilding houses. It can take **years** before things get back to **normal**.
- People have a range of views on how to help those living in poverty in other situations:

> Giving **money** (e.g. benefits or donations) to people in poverty makes them too **reliant** on that money — they don't **help themselves** get out of poverty as they prefer to keep **receiving** the money.

 vs.

> People living in poverty need **financial help**, because **not** giving it to them means they might not be able to **eat** or **heat** their home.

> It's people's **own responsibility** to get out of poverty — they should work **harder** and use money more **responsibly**.

 vs.

> Poverty is a result of **many factors**, and many people do **work hard**. Society should help those who face **many issues** such as **illness**, or a **lack of skills** or **opportunities**.

> In 2016, 1 in 8 people employed in the UK were living in poverty (source Joseph Rowntree Foundation, 2016).

- **Charities** often try to help people learn **new skills** on top of giving them **money** or **food**.

> **Utilitarian ethics** say the **correct** course of action is the one which has the **largest** balance of **good** against **bad** outcomes for those involved. Utilitarians often think people with **excess wealth** should give to people with **less wealth**. But if the money could be spent on **another** cause that would have a **greater benefit** (e.g. preventing more climate change), then giving the money to people **in poverty** would be **wrong**.

Wealth and Poverty

There are other problems often linked with poverty

Excessive Interest on Loans

- People sometimes need **extra money**, e.g. to pay for something **unexpected**, or just to afford **food** until the **next payday**. One **way** of covering this is to take out a **loan**. A quick and seemingly easy way to do so is to borrow from a **money lender**, but **money lenders** often practise **usury**. People might take out **small** loans, but they soon become so **big** that they **can't repay** them.
- This was a **big** problem in the UK, so the **government** introduced some **regulations** to **limit** how much people have to **repay**. Now, people don't have to repay more than **twice** what they borrowed.

usury
lending money at rates that go up to thousands of percent of interest

People-trafficking

- People living in poverty are often more **vulnerable** to **people-trafficking**. People are forced to work for **little** or **no** money, after they've been transferred to a **new place** (often **abroad**) by the **traffickers**.
- People are often persuaded to move **willingly** by the promise of a **better life** elsewhere, but once they get there the traffickers **force** them to work to pay back the money they **owe** for the **move**.

How money is used is important in Christianity and Islam

Christians believe it's important not to be **fixated** on wealth. Both Christians and Muslims believe that it's what you **do** with your **money** that **counts**, as summarised in the table below.

> **"You cannot serve both God and Money."**
> *Matthew 6:24 NIV*

	CHRISTIANITY	ISLAM
Uses of money	• People with lots of wealth should use it to help others who are less well off. • They also try to avoid using their money in a way that harms others.	• Muslims shouldn't use money in ways that harm people — Islamic law says Muslims shouldn't harm others.
Ways of earning money	• Many Christians think money should only be earned in moral ways, not in ways that might harm others, such as working for arms manufacturers or running a business that pays people unfair wages.	• Islam forbids alcohol, so it's seen as immoral to make money from it. • Islam is often focused on sexual modesty, so profiting from sex is forbidden (either directly or indirectly, e.g. sexually suggestive adverts).

Usury	• Usury is viewed as harming others.
	  • The Church of England has launched an initiative to combat lenders who charge lots of interest. The Church is offering workshops to educate people about money matters, as well as promoting credit unions, which lend money at low rates of interest.
		• Qur'an 2:275 says *"Allah ... has forbidden interest"* and that those who charge it will go to jahannam (hell). In Islam, money doesn't have a value in itself, so it shouldn't be used to make more money. This stops richer people profiting from poorer people, and ensures wealth is spread more fairly.
		  • Muslims use Islamic bank accounts and run businesses that don't involve charging interest.

Both faiths work to end people-trafficking

- Religious leaders have created the Global Freedom Network. This is an organisation which aims to end slavery. It works with governments to get them to pass laws to combat slavery and people-trafficking.
- The Church of England campaigned for the Modern Slavery Act, to protect victims of people-trafficking.

Wealth and Poverty

Charity *is important to* Christians

- Giving to **charity** and **helping** others is **important** to many **Christians**, following the teaching to *"Love your neighbour"* (Mark 12:31 NIV).
- It's important to give in a way that helps people to help **themselves** — the **parable** of the **talents** (Matthew 25:14-30) says those who make **most** of what they **have** are **rewarded**.
- **Christians** should give to **charity** as part of their **faith**. There are many **Christian** charities — see p.22.

> **"If anyone has material possessions and sees a brother or sister in need but has no pity on them, how can the love of God be in that person?"** *1 John 3:17 NIV*

Checking your donation's gone to a worthy cause is a good idea...

- It's best to give donations **quietly** and **without boasting** about it:

> **"...when you give to the needy, do not announce it with trumpets..."** *Matthew 6:2 NIV*

For more teachings on wealth, see p.102 and 105.

- **How much** you give **isn't** important — what's important is giving as **much** as you **can**.

> Jesus taught that a **poor woman** giving a **small** amount of money she couldn't **afford to lose** was **more** important than **rich** people giving **large** sums they could **easily do without**.

- Over **7500** churches are involved with the **Fairtrade** movement. For more on **Christian charities**, see p.22.

Charity *is one of the* Five Pillars *of Islam*

Charity plays an **important role** in Islam. Muslims think **wealth** is given to people by **Allah**, so they should use it to **help** others. Being **wealthy** or **poor** is Allah's **test** of people — they should try to help **themselves** or **others**, depending on the **situation**.

> **"A man is not a believer who fills his stomach while his neighbour is hungry."** *Al-Adab al-Mufrad 6:112 (collection of hadith)*

Zakah *is charity in the form of financial aid*

- **Zakah** is one of the **five pillars** of Islam, which every Muslim has to **follow**.
- With **zakah**, **2.5%** of your yearly **wealth** should be given as **charity**, unless your wealth is below a minimum threshold. It's usually given to **charities** or **mosques**, or to Muslims who are **less well off**.

> **"righteousness is [in] one who ... gives zakah"** *Qur'an 2:177*

Sadaqah *is another kind of charity*

- **Sadaqah** includes a **wide range** of charitable acts, from simply **smiling** at someone to **cheer** them up, to giving **money** to help those in **need**. Sadaqah is seen as a **duty**, but it involves **any amount** of effort, time or money — it's up to the individual to decide how much they do.
- There's a particular **emphasis** on 'ongoing charity' — **actions** that will have a **long-term effect**. It's seen as best to help people become able to **support** themselves, rather than **relying** on **donations**. This means the benefits of sadaqah are **long-lasting** and help the **community** — known as **sustainable development**.

There are Islamic **charities** that help people **globally** and in the UK, including **Muslim Aid** and **Islamic Aid**.

Muslim Aid	- Muslim Aid provides **disaster relief** and **development aid** around the world.
	- The charity works in over **70** countries.
	- It provides not only initial **emergency** aid after a **war** or **natural disaster**, but **ongoing** help. This help includes building new **housing**, **sanitation** and **schools**, and offering interest-free loans to help **start-up businesses**.

| Islamic Aid | - Islamic Aid is an **international** organisation dedicated to **reducing poverty** and **deprivation**. |
| | - It focuses on a **long-term** approach to helping communities and employs people from the **communities** it works in. |

I hope you feel richer (in knowledge) after these pages...

Make sure you've learnt the technical terms for different kinds of charitable acts, such as zakah.

Revision Summary

Now here's the fun bit — let's see if you can remember what you've just read in the section. The questions below will give you an idea of what the exam will be like and how much you'll need to write.

If you're struggling with anything, have another read of the section and give the questions another go once you've re-read it. When you're happy you can answer a question, tick it off.

Keep an eye out for the questions that give you extra marks for spelling, punctuation and grammar — you'll need to check your writing thoroughly for those.

Let's start off with some straightforward 1 mark multiple choice questions.

1) Which of the following is prejudice against people who are homosexual?
    a) Sexism   b) Homophobia   c) Racism   d) Heterosexuality

2) Which of the following people fought against apartheid in South Africa?
    a) Malcolm X   b) Muhammad   c) Desmond Tutu   d) Jesus

3) Which of the following means equality of rights and opportunities?
    a) Social justice   b) Freedom of belief   c) Discrimination   d) Gender inequality

4) Which of the following is the principle the Fairtrade Foundation campaigns for?
    a) Wealth inequality   b) Utilitarian ethics   c) Low pay   d) Fair pay

Right, now you need to write a bit. These are worth 2 marks, so give two short points.

5) Give two forms of prejudice.

6) Give two examples of human rights.

7) Give two religious beliefs about working for social justice.

8) Give two ways religious believers are working to combat people-trafficking.

Now on to 4 marks. You still need to make two points, but develop them more to get two marks for each. You need to write about the views of one or more religions.

9) Explain two similar religious beliefs about racism.

10) Explain two contrasting religious beliefs about homosexuality.

11) Explain two similar religious beliefs about human rights.

> Make sure your longer answers are clear by structuring your answer well and writing clear points.

For this question, you must refer to the main religious tradition in the UK and at least one other religious viewpoint. This question is worth 4 marks.

12) Explain two contrasting beliefs about the status of women in religion.

5 marks available for these questions. For top marks, you need to refer to religious texts.

13) Explain two religious beliefs about equality.

14) Explain two religious beliefs about freedom of belief.

15) Explain two religious beliefs about charging interest.

16) Explain two religious beliefs about giving to charity.

And... the 12 mark question, which has an additional 3 marks available for spelling, grammar and punctuation. Try using the bullet points in the question to make a plan before you begin — you'll have to include everything the bullet points ask for in your answer, and a plan will help you remember it all. Have a good think about arguments for and against the statement before you begin.

17) 'A religious believer can only truly be righteous if they are poor.'
    Evaluate this statement.
    Your answer should include the following:
    • religious arguments that support the statement
    • religious arguments that disagree with the statement
    • a conclusion

> Have a look at the 'Do Well in Your Exam' section for help with writing essays.

Theme F — Religion, Human Rights and Social Justice

The Start of Jesus's Ministry

In this section, the numbers in the subheadings give the reference for the Gospel extract you need to study.

John the Baptist baptised people in the River Jordan (1:1-8)

- Mark **doesn't** have any stories about **Jesus's birth** — he starts with the story of **John the Baptist**.

- Mark quotes from the Old Testament, where God says he will send a messenger to *"Prepare the way for the Lord"* (Mark 1:3 NIV). Mark says that **John** was this messenger, preparing for the coming Messiah.

- John baptised people in the **River Jordan** by **total immersion**.

 The water symbolises being cleansed of their sins — they had repented and now wanted to live good lives.

 The River Jordan was also symbolic to these people — in the Old Testament, the Israelites crossed the River Jordan to enter the Promised Land.

The people baptised in the river by John entered the new 'Promised Land' of **God's kingdom**.

- John predicted someone **greater** would come to **baptise** people, this time with the Holy Spirit:

> **"After me comes the one more powerful than I, the straps of whose sandals I am not worthy to stoop down and untie. I baptise you with water, but he will baptise you with the Holy Spirit."** *Mark 1:7-8 NIV*

The Old Testament prophet Joel had predicted the Holy Spirit would be present on Earth when the Messiah came (Joel 2). So John was saying the Messiah was coming — this Messiah was Jesus.

Jesus was baptised by John and tempted by Satan (1:9-13)

- **Jesus** was **baptised** in the River Jordan by John — this marked the **beginning** of Jesus's **ministry**. The **Holy Spirit** appeared as Jesus was being baptised and he heard a **voice** from **heaven**:

> **"...he saw heaven being torn open and the Spirit descending on him like a dove."** *Mark 1:10 NIV*

> **"You are my Son, whom I love; with you I am well pleased"** *Mark 1:11 NIV*

God's words show how important Jesus is to him — this was God giving Jesus his mission.

Baptism is still **important** to Christians **today** — it's how people are **welcomed** into the **Church** (see p.14).

- Then the Holy Spirit made Jesus go out into the **desert**:

> **"...he was in the wilderness for forty days, being tempted by Satan... angels attended him."** *Mark 1:13 NIV*

Jesus was being tested — Satan, God's archenemy, was trying to make Jesus sin and go against God. But Jesus didn't give in to Satan, which shows his power. God's love for Jesus is demonstrated by the way he sent his messengers, the angels, to care for him.

Christians believe they also will be **tested** and **tempted**. But with **God's help**, they can **get through** it just like Jesus did. Christians remember Jesus's struggle during **Lent** (see p.19) — a period which tests their ability to **overcome temptation**.

Jesus's titles show how important he is

Mark calls Jesus *"the Messiah, the Son of God"* (Mark 1:1 NIV). Titles such as these explain his role.

SON OF GOD	MESSIAH
By calling Jesus the 'Son of God', Mark means Jesus is God's special one — he has a unique relationship to God, and God gave him a unique mission. The title would have stressed Jesus's importance to 1st century Jews — it was used in the Old Testament for kings, and also for the whole nation of Israel.	Messiah means 'anointed one' in Hebrew (Mark also uses 'Christ', which is the Greek translation). It also used to be given to the kings of Israel. It later came to mean a heavenly figure who would come to save the Jews from their enemies — Mark believed Jesus was this saviour. The Messiah was often expected as a military figure, but since Jesus wasn't, he didn't specifically use the term for himself (see p.94).

 EXAM TIP

Don't mix up John the Baptist and John the disciple...

This section covers the Gospel of Mark in depth, and for the exam you'll need to know the key passages like the back of your hand. So get a cup of tea, sit down and read through them all.

Jesus's Miracles

At the start of Jesus's ministry, he performed many **miracles** as he travelled around teaching.

Jesus forgave and healed a paralysed man (2:1-12)

- When Jesus was teaching in a **crowded house**, some men carried a **paralysed man** to him. Because there were so many people, there was no way in, so they had to find an **alternative**:

> "...they made an opening in the roof above Jesus... and then lowered the mat the man was lying on. When Jesus saw their faith, he said to the paralysed man, 'Son, your sins are forgiven'. " *Mark 2:4-5 NIV*

Jesus was impressed by their strong **faith**, but didn't immediately heal the man — he **first** forgave his **sins**.

- There were people there who were **shocked** by what Jesus did:

> "Why does this fellow talk like that? He's blaspheming! Who can forgive sins but God alone?" *Mark 2:7 NIV*

They believed that only **God** could forgive sins — Jesus was **falsely** claiming **God's authority**.

- Jesus then **healed** the man, who was able to **walk** out of the room.
- The people *"praised God, saying, 'We have never seen anything like this!' "* (**Mark 2:12 NIV**). They realised that **Jesus's power** must have come from **God**.

> The story shows **modern Christians** that they must put their **faith** in **Jesus's power**. By demonstrating his **power** through **healing**, Jesus showed he also must be **powerful** enough to **forgive sins**. But to him, forgiving sins was more **important**.

> "But I want you to know that the **Son of Man** has authority on earth to forgive sins." *Mark 2:10 NIV*

Christians have a range of views on the meaning of this story

Some believe the story may be understood **literally**, whereas others think it's **symbolic**:

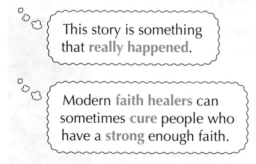

This story is something that **really happened**.

Modern **faith healers** can sometimes **cure** people who have a **strong** enough faith.

The story is a **metaphor** that shows how Jesus is **powerful** enough to heal people **spiritually**, freeing them from their sins.

Jesus uses the title 'Son of Man' in this passage

- The 'Son of Man' is a title that Jesus often uses when referring to **himself**.
- There are **various interpretations** of what the title means:

Daniel 7:13-14 talks about the Son of Man as a powerful, heavenly figure.

In Jesus's language, **Aramaic**, it was the normal way of talking about **yourself**, like using 'I'.

It shows Jesus's **humanity**.

Jesus's Miracles

Jesus brought a girl back to life (5:21-24 and 5:35-43)

- **Jairus**, a synagogue leader, **begged** Jesus to help his **dying daughter**.

> "My little daughter is dying. Please come and put your hands on her so that she will be healed and live." *Mark 5:23 NIV*

- But the girl **died** while Jesus was on his way. However, Jesus told Jairus to have **faith**. He'd **already** shown his faith by going to Jesus, but Jesus **encouraged** even **greater faith**.

- When Jesus saw the girl:

> "He took her by the hand and said to her... 'Little girl, I say to you, get up!' " *Mark 5:41 NIV*

The words 'little girl' are translated from a phrase in Aramaic which literally means 'little lamb', showing Jesus's care for the child.

- The girl was brought **back to life**, and began to **move** around.

- Jesus told them **not** to mention what had happened.

Jesus was rejected in his hometown (6:1-6)

- After being away from his hometown of Nazareth, Jesus **returned** in his new role and started teaching in the synagogue.

- But the people there knew him as their carpenter, the son of Mary. They **didn't believe** he could be God's chosen one.

- Jesus said:

> "He could not do any miracles there, except lay his hands on a few people who were ill and heal them. He was amazed at their lack of faith." *Mark 6:5-6 NIV*

> "A prophet is not without honour except in his own town, among his relatives and in his own home." *Mark 6:4 NIV*

Jesus previously said the disciples were his true relatives.

Many Christians were (and sometimes still are) **misunderstood** and **rejected** by their **families**. They can **take heart** from the fact that it happened to **Jesus** too.

Jesus miraculously fed 5000 people (6:30-44)

- A **large crowd** followed Jesus to an isolated place, so he decided to **teach** them. As it got late, Jesus instructed his **disciples** to **feed** the people, but they only had **five loaves** of bread and **two fish**.

- Jesus manages to make the little food they have feed **everyone** — there were at least **5000 people** there but there was still lots **left over**.

> "Taking the five loaves and the two fish and looking up to heaven, he gave thanks and broke the loaves. Then he gave them to his disciples to distribute to the people. He also divided the two fish among them all." *Mark 6:41 NIV*

This miracle is important for many reasons:

- It would have reminded **1st century Jews** of the Old Testament story where God fed the **Israelites** on miraculous manna (bread) while they were with **Moses** in the **wilderness**.

- For Christians today, it's a **reminder** of how Jesus also broke bread at the **Last Supper** — Christians are **fed spiritually** by Jesus when they remember this at the **Eucharist** (see p.97).

- It also reminds them to have **faith** that God will **look after** them. He can deal with **big problems** and do great things with the **small offerings** that they make in their lives.

- The story appears in **all four Gospels** — Christians think this makes it likely that it's **true**.

Jesus's Miracles

Jesus restored sight to a blind man (10:46-52)

- Jesus and his followers came across Bartimaeus, a blind man, begging at the side of the road.

- He called out "*Jesus, Son of David, have mercy on me!*" (Mark 10:47 NIV) and told Jesus he wanted to be able to see. Jesus healed him:

> " '*Go... your faith has healed you.*' Immediately he received his sight and followed Jesus along the road" *Mark 10:52 NIV*

- Bartimaeus threw away his cloak before going to Jesus. He would have used it to catch coins that people tossed to him, so he abandoned his means of livelihood to follow Jesus, just like the other disciples.

This reminds Christians today that they should focus more on their faith than on worldly goods.

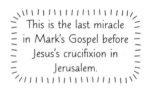 Many Christians interpret this story as meaning that they're spiritually blind without Jesus, but if they have faith and follow him, their eyes will be opened to how they should live their lives.

SON OF DAVID
- The title 'Son of David' was used in this story.
- David was the greatest of the kings of Israel in the Old Testament, so people who used this title saw Jesus as a new king who would rule justly, like David did.
- Also, the Messiah was prophesied to be David's descendant, so by using this title, people acknowledge Jesus as the Messiah.

This is the last miracle in Mark's Gospel before Jesus's crucifixion in Jerusalem.

The miracle stories tell us a lot about Jesus

- The miracles in Mark's Gospel show how Jesus had God's power. They also show his compassion for people who were suffering or in need.

- Although Mark focuses on Jesus's actions in these stories, they also show Jesus as a popular teacher. Mark portrays how Jesus travelled around teaching, usually attracting huge crowds.

The miracle stories can be interpreted in different ways

By Christians...

Jesus's miracles actually happened.

They're metaphors that symbolise a spiritual truth.

Some Christians accept both these meanings.

And by non-religious people...

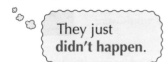

They just didn't happen.

There are ways to explain the events rationally using science.

Learn this and you won't need a miracle to pass the exam...

These stories show Christians how they should follow Jesus and have faith in their everyday lives. See if you can jot down a quick summary of each miracle, and why they're important for modern-day Christians.

Theme G — St Mark's Gospel: the Life of Jesus

The Later Ministry of Jesus

It's not until the **second half** of Mark's Gospel that Jesus is recognised as the **Messiah**.

Jesus was declared the Messiah and predicted his death (8:27-33)

This is an important **turning point** in Mark's Gospel. Jesus's **ministry** in Galilee had **finished**, and he was starting to move towards **Jerusalem**, where he knew he would **die**.

- Jesus and his disciples were travelling near the town Caesarea Philippi when he asked them, *"Who do people say I am?"*. They told him: *"Some say John the Baptist; others say Elijah; and still others, one of the prophets"* (Mark 8:27-28 NIV).

  > John the Baptist had been executed, so some people thought he'd come back from the dead in Jesus.

- So far, **no-one** had said that Jesus was the **Messiah**. But when Jesus asked his disciples who he was, **Peter** replied: *"You are the Messiah"* (Mark 8:29 NIV).

- But Peter had **misunderstood** Jesus's real mission — he may have thought the Messiah would be a **political** or **military** figure (see p.90).

- Jesus then tells them about how he would **suffer** and **die** — but would come back to **life**:

  > **"...the Son of Man must suffer many things and be rejected by the elders, the chief priests and the teachers of the law... he must be killed and after three days rise again."** *Mark 8:31 NIV*

- Peter **told him off**. He thought it was **impossible** for the Messiah to **die**, so Jesus must be **wrong**.

- Jesus replied: *" 'Get behind me, Satan! ... You do not have in mind the concerns of God, but merely human concerns' "* (Mark 8:33 NIV).

  > Jesus was criticising Peter for trying to tempt him away from his true mission from God, just as Satan had tempted Jesus in the wilderness. However, God's plan for salvation involved Jesus being crucified.

Jesus's true nature was shown to the disciples (9:2-9)

- Jesus went up a **mountain** with Peter, James and John — the three disciples he was **closest** to. Then, his **appearance** changed:

  > **"His clothes became dazzling white... And there appeared before them Elijah and Moses, who were talking with Jesus."** *Mark 9:3-4 NIV*

  > Elijah and Moses were two of the greatest figures of the Old Testament. Moses gave Jews the Law and Elijah was the greatest of the Prophets. The way that they appeared with Jesus showed he was the Messiah in the Old Testament prophecies.

- This is called 'the **transfiguration**'. The disciples were shown the true **divine nature** behind Jesus's **normal appearance**.

- **God** spoke:

  > **"...a cloud appeared and covered them, and a voice came from the cloud: 'This is my son, whom I love. Listen to him!' "** *Mark 9:7 NIV*

  > This demonstrates how important Jesus's words were.

- On the way down, Jesus **forbade** them to speak about it until he had **come back** from the **dead**.

- The story reveals just how **important** Jesus was, and the **power** that God had given him.

 EXAM QUESTION

It's time to show your true nature as a dedicated student...

Give two reasons why Peter was angry when Jesus told the disciples he would die. [2]

The Later Ministry of Jesus

The Messianic Secret is a big part of Mark's Gospel

- Jesus told his disciples **not** to **tell** anyone that he was the **Messiah**.
  The real **nature** of Jesus's **messiahship** is only truly **understood** after the resurrection
  — this is the **Messianic Secret** in Mark.

- This has many parts:

  > For example, Jesus told people **not** to talk about the **miracles** he performed, and his teachings in the form of parables could be **difficult** to **understand** (see p.101-102).

- He may have wanted to keep his messiahship a **secret** in case it was **misunderstood**.

  Although Jesus tried to keep it a secret, by the time he got to Jerusalem, people were calling him the Messiah.

Jesus predicted his death and resurrection again (10:32-34)

- While going to Jerusalem, Jesus again told the disciples he would be killed, but would rise from the grave.

- This was the third time he predicted his death — he gave more detail than before:

  > "...the Son of Man will be delivered over to the chief priests and the teachers of the law. They will condemn him to death and will hand him over to the Gentiles, who will mock him and spit on him, flog him and kill him. Three days later he will rise." Mark 10:33-34 NIV

The Gentiles were the Romans — the Jews couldn't execute people because the Romans ruled over them, so they would have to give Jesus to the Romans.

This was one of his 'passion predictions' — Jesus's suffering and death are called the 'passion'.

- The things Jesus predicted later happened (see p.97-99). Mark presents the events as the fulfilment of Jesus's prophecy, and as part of the divine plan.

- The crucifixion came as a devastating shock to the disciples. But eventually they came to understand that it was an essential part of God's plan, not a defeat. Mark shows that Jesus understood this in advance and continued to Jerusalem despite knowing what awaited him.

It's no secret that Jesus's ministry could be in the exam...

Jesus did a lot during his time on Earth, so it might be easy to get it all jumbled up. Try drawing a timeline of the events described over the last few pages, to help you remember what happened and when. Add some notes on the main points of each story, and you'll be set for the exam.

The Later Ministry of Jesus

Jesus told his disciples about serving others (10:35-45)

- **James** and **John** asked to sit on Jesus's **right** and **left sides** when he returned to **heaven** in **glory**. They wanted to be the **closest** to Jesus, and the **most important**.

- Jesus asked if they would be willing to go through the **trials** he'd suffer. They said yes. Jesus said they'd **suffer**, but the **places** by his side were **decided by God**.

  > **"Can you drink the cup I drink..."**
  > *Mark 10:38 NIV*

- The **other disciples** were **angry** that James and John wanted to be more important than them. Jesus said:

  > **"...whoever wants to become great among you must be your servant, and whoever wants to be first must be slave of all. For even the Son of Man did not come to be served, but to serve, and to give his life as a ransom for many."** *Mark 10:43-45 NIV*

  Only people who were humble and served others on Earth would be rewarded in heaven. Jesus would later serve humanity by dying so that they would be reconciled with God (see p.11).

Many Christians try to **serve** others, e.g. through their **job** or by **dedicating** themselves to the **Church**.

Jesus entered Jerusalem as a new king (11:1-11)

- Jesus and his disciples were getting **near** to **Jerusalem** — the **holy city** where **David** and the other kings had reigned. Jesus told two disciples to bring him a young **donkey** (a colt), which Jesus rode.

- In the Old Testament, the **Messiah** was predicted to enter Jerusalem on a **donkey** (Zechariah 9:9).
- Riding in on a donkey showed Jesus's **humility** and **peaceful** nature, something Christians should try to **follow**.

- Some people laid **cloaks** and **branches** across Jesus's path, which showed how **respected** he was.

- As he rode into Jerusalem, they cried:

  > **"Hosanna! Blessed is he who comes in the name of the Lord! Blessed is the coming kingdom of our father David!"** (Mark 11:9-10 NIV).

  Hosanna means 'save now' — the people of Jerusalem believed that Jesus was the Messiah, and was there to help them.

- Jesus is celebrated as David's successor — the new **messianic king**. This follows straight after Bartimaeus called him 'Son of David' (see p.93).

Christians remember this event on **Palm Sunday**, named after the branches people used. They're reminded of how Jesus was **proclaimed** as the **saviour**, and also of his **humility**. But Christians today **know** how the crowd soon **turned against** Jesus. They must be **careful** to keep their **faith** in him.

Serving others is important, so here's something for you...

See if you can summarise the events that took place in the later stages of Jesus's ministry. Extra points if you can back them up with specific references to Mark's Gospel.

The Final Days in Jerusalem

Jesus had arrived in **Jerusalem**, and he knew that this was where he would be **betrayed** by one of his disciples.

Jesus ate with his disciples at the *Last Supper (14:12-26)*

- Jesus and the disciples ate the **Passover meal** together — this is known as the **Last Supper**.

  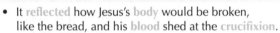

  > Passover is the Jewish festival that **remembers** the Jews' **escape** from **slavery** in Egypt. Christians believe that the death of Jesus also **rescues** people from sin and death.

- At the meal, Jesus predicted that one of the disciples would **betray** him. They all denied it.

  > **"Truly I tell you, one of you will betray me — one who is eating with me"** *Mark 14:18 NIV*

- He **divided** up some **bread** and passed it to **everyone**, saying, *"Take it; this is my body"* (Mark 14:22 NIV). Then he **passed** around a cup of **wine**, saying *"This is my blood of the covenant, which is poured out for many"* (Mark 14:24 NIV).

  - It reflected how Jesus's body would be broken, like the bread, and his blood shed at the crucifixion.
  - 'Covenant' referred to the agreement God made with the Jews in the Old Testament.
  - Jesus was saying that his life and death created a new relationship with God.

- Jesus also said, *"...I will not drink again from the fruit of the vine until that day when I drink it new in the kingdom of God"* (Mark 14:25 NIV). He knew that his **death** was **near**.

  Jesus's actions are still very important to Christians today — they re-enact them in the Eucharist. But there are different beliefs about what Jesus's words meant.
  - Some believe the bread and wine had literally become his body and blood, whereas others think he meant that they just represented them.
  - This is why the Eucharist is celebrated in different ways — read the third section of p.14 for more about this.

Jesus was *arrested* in the Garden of Gethsemane (14:32-52)

- Jesus told the disciples to **keep watch** as he **prayed** in the **Garden of Gethsemane**, but they fell asleep.
- Jesus asked **God** if he could **avoid** what was coming, but then he **submitted** to **God's will**.

  > **"Abba, Father... everything is possible for you. Take this cup from me. Yet not what I will, but what you will."** *Mark 14:36 NIV*

  Jesus was afraid to go through with the suffering ahead — this shows that he was a real human being. But his obedience to God is an example for Christians. Early Christians followed his example in trusting God, even when persecuted.

- Then **Judas** (one of the disciples) arrived with the chief priests' **armed men**. He **betrayed** Jesus with a **kiss**.

  > **"The one I kiss is the man; arrest him and lead him away under guard"** *Mark 14:44 NIV*

  Jesus was placed under **arrest** by the men.

- One of the **disciples** *"drew his sword and struck the servant of the high priest, cutting off his ear"* (Mark 14:47 NIV). Then, the disciples all **ran away**.

- Jesus **questioned** why he was being **captured** — he asked if they thought he was leading a **rebellion**, which he **wasn't**. But he said, *"the Scriptures must be fulfilled"* (Mark 14:49 NIV).

EXAM QUESTION

This was just the beginning of Jesus's suffering...

Give two reasons why Jesus's words and actions in the Garden of Gethsemane are important. [2]

The Final Days in Jerusalem

Jesus was *tried by the Jewish authorities* (14:53, 57-65)

- Jesus was tried before the Jewish high priest.
- The high priest asked him: *"Are you the Messiah, the Son of the Blessed One?"* (Mark 14:61 NIV).
- Jesus replied *"I am... And you will see the Son of Man sitting at the right hand of the Mighty One and coming on the clouds of heaven"* (Mark 14:62 NIV).
- Witnesses gave false evidence against him, and their stories didn't agree. But Jesus was found guilty of blasphemy (because they believed he was falsely claiming to be divine) — a crime carrying the death penalty. He had to be handed to the Romans for his punishment.

> blasphemy
> *insulting or showing disrespect to God or other aspects of religion*

Jesus was *sentenced to death by the Roman governor* (15:1-15)

- Jesus was tried before the **Roman governor**, **Pilate**, the next day. Blasphemy **wasn't** a crime to the Romans, but he could have been a **political** threat. Pilate asked Jesus if he was the **king of the Jews**. He answered *"You have said so"* (Mark 15:2 NIV). He **didn't defend** himself — he **submitted** to God's plan.
- Pilate **realised** Jesus wasn't really a threat — the priests had handed him over because they **didn't** like him. Since a prisoner was released every **Passover**, Pilate offered to **release** Jesus.
- But the chief priests got the **people** to ask for **Barabbas**, a murderer, instead. When Pilate asked about Jesus they said *"Crucify him!"* (Mark 15:13 NIV). So Jesus was **flogged** and sent to be **crucified**.

Jesus was *crucified, died and was buried* (15:21-47)

- **Simon of Cyrene** was made to **carry** Jesus's **cross** to **Golgotha** ('the place of the skull').

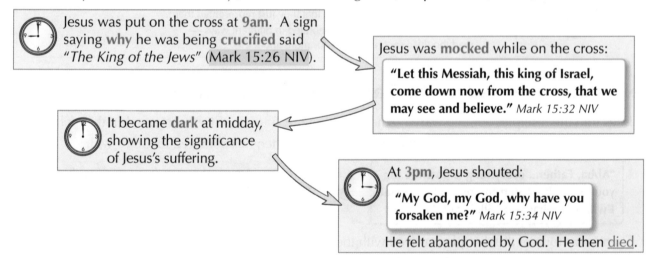

Jesus was put on the cross at **9am**. A sign saying **why** he was being **crucified** said *"The King of the Jews"* (Mark 15:26 NIV).

Jesus was **mocked** while on the cross:

> **"Let this Messiah, this king of Israel, come down now from the cross, that we may see and believe."** *Mark 15:32 NIV*

It became **dark** at midday, showing the significance of Jesus's suffering.

At **3pm**, Jesus shouted:

> **"My God, my God, why have you forsaken me?"** *Mark 15:34 NIV*

He felt abandoned by God. He then <u>died</u>.

- As Jesus **died**, the temple **curtain ripped** in two.

This curtain hid the Holy of Holies — a special room inside the temple where God was believed to be present, and only the high priest could enter. This showed that everyone now had access to God.

- The Roman **soldier** who saw Jesus die said *"Surely this man was the Son of God!"* (Mark 15:39 NIV). He **recognised** who Jesus was, but the Jewish leaders **didn't**.
- **Joseph of Arimathea** was given Jesus's **body** by Pilate. He *"bought some linen cloth, took down the body, wrapped it in the linen, and placed it in a tomb cut out of rock"* (Mark 15:46 NIV).

> Many Christians believe that Jesus's death **saved mankind** and **repaired** the **relationship** with God. But there are **various views** about the crucifixion — read the **first section of** p.11 for more detail.

The Final Days in Jerusalem

Jesus's tomb was found empty (16:1-8)

- Three women went to Jesus's tomb on **Sunday morning**, but they found the stone **rolled back** and the tomb **empty**. There they saw a **man** in white (an **angel**). He told them *"He has risen! He is not here"* (Mark 16:6 NIV). He told them to tell the disciples that Jesus would meet them in **Galilee**.

- The women left the tomb, **frightened** and **confused** by what they saw. They **didn't** tell anyone about it.

- Some early Bibles **finish** the story **here**, but later copies added **reports** of encounters with the **risen Jesus**.

- The resurrection turned **despair** to **hope** for the disciples. Everything **hadn't** gone **wrong** — the crucifixion was part of **God's plan**.

> The resurrection is **important** to Christians for many reasons — read the box in the **middle of p.10**. It shows that **Jesus** really is **God's son**. It would also have given persecuted early Christians hope that there was something else beyond their suffering.

HOWEVER...

Many people believe the resurrection is scientifically impossible — they explain the empty tomb in other ways. But those who believe in the resurrection have arguments against these explanations.

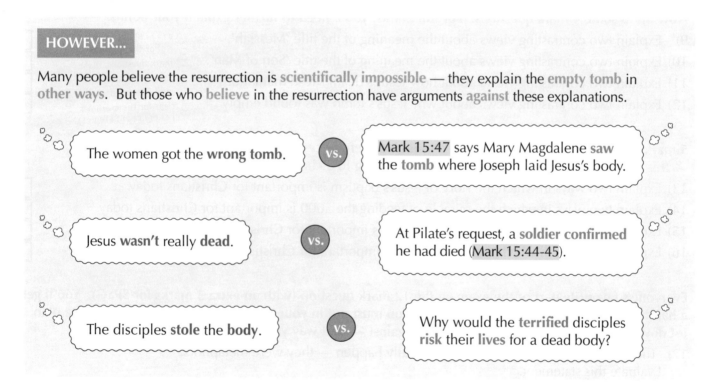

The women got the **wrong tomb**.	**vs.**	Mark 15:47 says Mary Magdalene **saw** the **tomb** where Joseph laid Jesus's body.
Jesus **wasn't** really **dead**.	**vs.**	At Pilate's request, a **soldier confirmed** he had died (Mark 15:44-45).
The disciples **stole** the **body**.	**vs.**	Why would the **terrified** disciples **risk** their **lives** for a dead body?

Luckily for you, there's more Mark in the next section...

Not only do you need to know what happened in the last few days of Jesus's life, but you also need to know what these events can mean to different Christians. Some things, like what Jesus says at the Last Supper, are interpreted in various ways, so make sure you learn the differences.

Revision Summary

That was quite a lot to take in there, so now try out these **questions** to see what you're **comfortable** with and what needs a **bit more work**. They're like the ones you'll be asked in the actual **exam**.

If there's anything you **can't** answer, **go back** through the section and have **another go** when you've re-read it. For some questions — you'll be told which ones — there are **extra marks** for **spelling, punctuation** and **grammar**, so check your writing carefully.

Nice and easy to start off with — some 1 mark multiple choice questions.

1) Which one of the following is <u>not</u> a title given to Jesus in Mark's Gospel?
   a) Son of God   b) Messiah   c) Son of Man   d) Prophet

2) Which of these men did Jesus help to see?
   a) Bartimaeus   b) Jairus   c) Elijah   d) Pilate

3) Which of the disciples said that Jesus was the Messiah at Caesarea Philippi?
   a) James   b) John   c) Peter   d) Judas

4) At which of these places was Jesus crucified?
   a) Nazareth   b) Gethsemane   c) Golgotha   d) Jericho

Let's up the ante. 2 marks available per question, 2 short points to get them.

5) Give two examples of healing miracles performed by Jesus.

6) Give two reasons why Christians believe they should serve others.

7) Give two ways that Jesus kept his messiahship a secret.

8) Give two predictions Jesus made at the Last Supper.

Now on to some 4 mark questions. For full marks, you'll need to further explain your points.

9) Explain two contrasting views about the meaning of the title 'Messiah'.

10) Explain two contrasting views about the meaning of the title 'Son of Man'.

11) Explain two contrasting views about how Jesus's death saved mankind.

12) Explain two contrasting views about why Jesus's tomb was found empty.

> For the 4 and 5 mark questions, make sure your answer is well-organised so it's clear for the examiner.

5 marks for these questions. You'll have to include references to Mark's Gospel too — this could be by quoting, paraphrasing or referring to a chapter and verse.

13) Explain two ways in which the story of Jesus's baptism is important for Christians today.

14) Explain two ways in which the miracle of feeding the 5000 is important for Christians today.

15) Explain two ways in which Jesus's crucifixion is important for Christians today.

16) Explain two ways in which the resurrection is important for Christians today.

Everyone's favourite part of the exam — the 12 mark question (with an extra 3 marks for SPaG). You'll get a handy list of bullet points telling you what you must put in your answer, so use them to map out a plan. Jot down all the possible arguments for and against — that way you won't forget any.

17) 'The miracles Jesus performed didn't actually happen — they were metaphors.'
    Evaluate this statement.
    Your answer should include the following:
    • references to Mark's Gospel
    • religious arguments that support the statement
    • religious arguments that disagree with the statement
    • a conclusion
    You can also include non-religious points of view in your answer.

> 'References to Mark's Gospel' means either quotations, paraphrasing or chapter and verse references.

Theme G — St Mark's Gospel: the Life of Jesus

The Kingdom of God

This section looks at Mark's Gospel and the **kingdom of God**, and 1st century **society**, **faith** and **discipleship**.

The Kingdom of God can have different meanings

The kingdom of God is the **time** and **place** where **God rules**.
People will follow **God's will** and **live** according to it:

> "your kingdom come, your will be done, on earth as it is in heaven" *Matthew 6:10 NIV* ⟶ This is from the Lord's Prayer.

- It was a **central** part of **Jesus's preaching**. He explained that:

> "The time has come... The kingdom of God has come near. Repent and believe the good news!" *Mark 1:15 NIV*

- 'Kingdom of God' refers to **different times** and **places** in different passages of the Gospel:

The kingdom might exist as a state of being within the hearts and minds of individuals, or in the love and care shown within the community of believers. This applies both to Jesus's disciples and Christians now.	It can also refer to a physical kingdom in the future — God will establish a kingdom throughout the world, when Jesus returns in the Second Coming and the Last Judgement takes place (see p.8). Some think it may have already partly arrived in Jesus's healings and exorcisms (they show God's rule over sin and evil) but is still to arrive fully.

- Jesus explained what the kingdom of God is like by using **parables**.

> **parable**
> *a story about everyday life which contains a message about spiritual truth*

Parable of the sower — people react differently (4:1-9, 14-20)

Jesus told a story about a farmer who went to sow seeds in his field, and the seeds fell in different places. What happens to the seeds represents how people respond differently to Jesus's teaching.

Some of the seed *"fell along the path, and the birds came and ate it up"* (Mark 4:4 NIV). The birds are a metaphor for **Satan** — it's **easy** for him to make people **forget** Jesus's teaching. These people **hear** the teaching, but **don't act** on it.

Some fell where there was **little soil**. Although they quickly **grew**, they **died** from exposure to the hot sun: *"they withered because they had no root"* (Mark 4:6 NIV). This represents people who **accept** Jesus's message, but **give up** when things get **difficult**.

Some *"fell among thorns, which grew up and choked the plants, so that they did not bear grain"* (Mark 4:7 NIV). These symbolise people who **accept** Jesus's message, but get **distracted** by other things, e.g. **money** and **greed**.

Some seed *"fell on good soil. It came up, grew and produced a crop..."* (Mark 4:8 NIV). This group refers to people who **understand** Jesus's teaching, and try to **live** their lives by it.

- Jesus told the disciples that *"The secret of the kingdom of God has been given to you"* (Mark 4:11 NIV).
- The parable shows that the kingdom of God is present through people who follow Jesus's teaching. It encourages Christians to spread Jesus's message, but to accept that people won't always respond.

Parable of the growing seed — symbol of the kingdom (4:26-29)

Jesus told people that the kingdom of God was like a farmer who sows seed in a field:

> "Night and day... the seed sprouts and grows, though he does not know how. All by itself the soil produces corn — first the stalk, then the ear, then the full grain in the ear. As soon as the corn is ripe, he puts the sickle to it, because the harvest has come." *Mark 4:27-29 NIV*

- The parable explains that the kingdom of God grows in a mysterious way. Christians might not understand how God is working, but they can be confident that he is.
- The harvest represents judgement at the end of time — when the kingdom of God will be fully established. Those who've followed God's ways will be harvested to live in the kingdom of God.

Parables about farming — the cream of the crop...

For all parables in this section, make sure you understand the meaning behind each one, what they meant to people back in the time of Jesus, and what they mean to Christians today.

The Kingdom of God

Jesus taught people to **focus less** on **material things** so they could be a part of the kingdom of God.

Parable of the mustard seed — the kingdom would grow (4:30-32)

Jesus explained:

> "[the kingdom of God] is like a mustard seed, which is the smallest of all seeds on earth. Yet when planted, it grows and becomes the largest of all garden plants... the birds can perch in its shade" *Mark 4:31-32 NIV*

Jesus was describing how the kingdom of God would grow. The parable portrays the kingdom as a community, rather than just individuals — it started with Jesus, but expanded to his first followers and then thousands of Christians.

 Early Christians found this encouraging. Although there weren't many of them, it told them one day their movement would be great. Birds were a Jewish symbol for Gentiles (non-Jews), so it also encouraged them to look for converts in the Gentile world too.

 Some modern Christians think the big plant refers to the Church. The Church is a large community which provides care and protection to anyone who needs it — like a large plant does to birds. Many believe it should work to create the kingdom of God on Earth.

A rich man is unwilling to give up his possessions (10:17-27)

- A **rich man** asked Jesus what he must do to get **eternal life**. Jesus reminded him of the **Ten Commandments**, but the man explained that he **already** followed them.
- Jesus told him to *"sell everything you have and give to the poor, and you will have treasure in heaven. Then come, follow me"* (Mark 10:21 NIV). This may mean follow his **teachings** — or leave his home and join Jesus, **travelling** around spreading God's word.
- The man left in **despair** because he **couldn't** bear to do that.
- Jesus said to his disciples that it's very **difficult** for the **rich** to get into the **kingdom of God**:

> "It is easier for a camel to go through the eye of a needle than for someone who is rich to enter the kingdom of God." *Mark 10:25 NIV*

 The 'eye' of a needle is the **small hole** which the **thread** is put through when sewing, so the saying means it's **almost impossible** for rich people to be **saved**. But Jesus does also say *"all things are possible with God"* (Mark 10:27 NIV).

 'The eye of the needle' may have been a **narrow gate** in **Jerusalem**. Camels loaded with goods needed to be **unloaded** to **pass** through. So **rich people** have to shed their **possessions** before they can enter the **kingdom of God**, like a camel had to shed its load to enter Jerusalem.

Jesus's teaching on wealth was very surprising

Jesus's teaching on wealth surprised 1st century Jews. They believed that wealth was a sign of God's approval. But Jesus saw wealth as an obstacle to serving God fully — his disciples left their homes and possessions behind to follow him. Modern Christians interpret Jesus's teaching in a variety of ways:

> It means people shouldn't be too attached to money or possessions, but should give generously to those in need.

> It only applied to the time when Jesus lived. Giving away all your money is unrealistic now when people need money to buy even the basics. In the 1st century, people were more self-sufficient.

> Jesus's words about wealth only applied to that man — other people have different problems to overcome. The key point is that God must be first in your life — not money or anything else.

> The teaching is just wrong. If everyone gave everything away, society would collapse. It also would mean neglecting your duty to your family.

Monks and nuns take the teaching quite literally — they give up all their possessions and take a vow of poverty.

Theme H — St Mark's Gospel as a Source of Religious, Moral and Spiritual Truths

The Kingdom of God

Jesus instructed his disciples to **love** other people. Not just their friends — **everyone**.

Jesus welcomes young children despite opposition (10:13-16)

People took their **children** to see Jesus so he could **bless** them.
The **disciples** tried to **stop** it, but Jesus **overruled** them, saying:

> "Let the little children come to me, and do not hinder them, for the kingdom of God belongs to such as these. Truly I tell you, anyone who will not receive the kingdom of God like a little child will never enter it." *Mark 10:14-15 NIV*

He meant that the kingdom of God was for people who accepted it with childlike joy — people who are completely open to embracing new things.

The kingdom here is a present reality in the hearts and minds of individuals who apply Jesus's teaching.

This encourages modern Christians to **accept** Jesus's **message** in this way, and to treat children with **love**.

Love God and love other people (12:28-34)

* The **Old Testament** contains hundreds of principles to follow (including the **Ten Commandments**).
* A teacher of religion asked Jesus which was the **greatest principle**. He chose **two**:

> "the Lord our God, the Lord is one. Love the Lord your God with all your heart and with all your soul and with all your mind and with all your strength." *Mark 12:29-30 NIV*

This is adapted from Deuteronomy 6:4-5. Jesus meant that God should be the thing you love most in life — nothing should be more important.

> "Love your neighbour as yourself." *Mark 12:31 NIV*

  * This is from Leviticus 19:18. Although Jesus used the same words, in Leviticus the rule only meant love your own people — fellow Jews. Non-Jews weren't included. Jesus expanded this rule to cover all human beings.
  * It is sometimes called the Golden Rule, and this part of the Gospel is still regarded as an important rule today. It is accepted by most secular (non-religious) people.

The teacher **approved** of Jesus's answer. So Jesus said he was **close** to the **kingdom of God**, as he had **accepted** the key messages of the kingdom.

* Many **non-Christians** regard Jesus as an **important teacher**, and a **good man**.
Lots of modern people are **inspired** by his example of **selfless love** and **forgiveness** of **enemies**.
* Many modern Christians agree that **loving God** and loving **other people** is the **essence** of Christianity.
Many Christians have **devoted** their lives to the **service** of **others** as a consequence,
e.g. **Mother Teresa** of Calcutta.

What if Jesus's teaching contradicts the law or government?

* Christians believe that Jesus's **character** and **life** show what **God** is like.
They try to **obey** his teachings and to **live** in the **same way** that he did.
* Most Christians believe they should keep the **laws** and **obey** the **government** of the country
they live in. But they believe it is **right** to **disobey** these if the laws or government are **wrong**.

> For example, lots of Christians **refused** to obey the government in **Nazi Germany** — many **hid** Jews from the **government** so that they wouldn't be **killed**.

You must(ard) learn all this — it could pop up in the exam...

Create a spider diagram about the kingdom of God. Include when and where people think it might happen, what it will be like and how to get to it. Bonus points for specific Gospel references.

People Disregarded by Society

Jesus made a point of welcoming and helping those who were excluded from normal society.

Outcasts were excluded from society for different reasons

Many people were outcasts in 1st century Jewish society. Other people didn't interact with them, and they were excluded from worship — so they were cut off from God as well as from other people:

- SINNERS — People who deliberately broke the laws which good Jews kept were outcasts. Jews considered these laws to be God-given, and obeying them was essential to remain part of God's people.
- The ILL and DISABLED — These people were sometimes seen as being punished by God for their sins. Some diseases were thought to be spread by physical contact, so sufferers were isolated to stop others from getting infected. Some were thought to make the sufferer ritually unclean, so they couldn't join in worship. Other people couldn't touch them, because that made them unclean too.
- GENTILES — Parts of the Old Testament told Jews not to have any contact with non-Jews, and this was taught by some rabbis at the time of Jesus. They weren't considered to be God's people.
- The POOR — Very poor people couldn't afford to buy the sacrifices needed for worship at the Temple in Jerusalem. These sacrifices were needed to cleanse their sins, so they remained sinful.
- TAX COLLECTORS — They worked for the occupying Romans, so they were considered traitors. They often collected more than necessary and kept the rest for themselves.

Jesus welcomed outcasts — so Christians must too

- Jesus showed that outcasts were welcome in the kingdom of God. He also welcomed women and children — they were considered less important than men at the time.
- Modern Christians are inspired by his compassion for outcasts, and so they welcome all types of people. They're encouraged to accept and love everyone, whatever their gender, race, religion or past behaviour.
- This attitude has gradually been built into the laws of our society. Discrimination (treating people badly) because of their gender or race is now illegal.

Jesus healed a leper and helped him back into society (1:40-45)

- A leper asked Jesus for help. He said *"If you are willing, you can make me clean"* (Mark 1:40 NIV).
- Jesus touched him (making himself 'unclean') and the leper was healed instantly. Jesus then told him to visit a priest and make the sacrifices needed to cleanse a leper and remove his impurity (only a priest could declare someone free of leprosy).
- Jesus told the man to keep it a secret — but he told everyone.

leper
a person suffering from leprosy

leprosy
a skin disease that can seriously harm or even kill people. People believed it was spread by touching, so lepers were driven out of their homes.

> Christians believe that they should follow Jesus's teachings and example.
> - Early Christians cared for the sick during epidemics, and founded many of the first hospitals in Europe.
> - Many modern Christians also care for the sick, despite the risks. They believe compassion matters more than their own lives, and the best thing they can do is follow Jesus's teaching.

Jesus chooses an outcast to be a disciple (2:13-17)

- Levi was a tax collector who became one of Jesus's disciples.

> *"...he saw Levi... sitting at the tax collector's booth. 'Follow me,' Jesus told him, and Levi got up and followed him."* Mark 2:14 NIV

- Jesus later went to Levi's house to eat — other outcasts were also there. Visiting Levi's house and eating with him was a sign of acceptance of these outcasts.
- Some people criticised Jesus for it, but he replied: *"It is not the healthy who need a doctor, but those who are ill. I have not come to call the righteous, but sinners"* (Mark 2:17 NIV).
- Jesus showed that God values compassion and helping those in trouble above punishment for wrongdoing.

Theme H — St Mark's Gospel as a Source of Religious, Moral and Spiritual Truths

People Disregarded by Society

Jesus healed the daughter of a Gentile woman (7:24-30)

- A **Greek** (sometimes called **Syro-Phoenician**) **woman** had a **daughter** who was possessed by a **demon**. The woman asked Jesus to **heal** her.
- Jesus **refused**. He compared **Jews** and **non-Jews** to the **children** and **dogs** in a family: *"...it is not right to take the children's bread and toss it to the dogs"* (Mark 7:27 NIV). He was telling her that his **mission** was to help the Jews **before** any non-Jews.
- The woman replied: *"Lord... even the dogs under the table eat the children's crumbs"* (Mark 7:28 NIV). Because of her **humility** and **faith**, Jesus **healed** her daughter.

> Most Jews in Jesus's time had **little** to do with **Gentiles**, but there were several stories about Jesus **helping** Gentiles who approached him. Some **Gentiles** started becoming **Christians** soon after **Jesus's death**. Jesus showed that people **shouldn't** be **discriminated** against because of their **race** or **religion**.

Jesus drove a demon from a boy (9:14-29)

- A man's son was **possessed** by a **spirit**. It affected him **physically**: *"...it throws him to the ground. He foams at the mouth, gnashes his teeth and becomes rigid"* (Mark 9:18 NIV).
- Jesus spoke **harshly** to everyone, calling them an *"unbelieving generation"* (Mark 9:19 NIV).
- The man asked Jesus for **help**. Jesus said, *"Everything is possible for one who believes"* (Mark 9:23 NIV). But the man admitted his **faith** was **weak**: *"I do believe; help me overcome my unbelief!"* (Mark 9:24 NIV).
- Jesus told the spirit to **leave** the boy and **never** return. It **screamed**, caused the boy to **shake** and then **left**. The boy lay **still**, as if he were **dead**. But Jesus held his **hand** and helped him **up** — he was **cured**.

> Now people would recognise that the boy had **epilepsy**. But 1st century Jews — including **Mark** when he was reporting these events — didn't know the **scientific** explanation for epilepsy. Illnesses were often blamed on **demon possession** and sufferers were **shunned**.

A poor widow gave all she had to the Temple (12:41-44)

- People were giving **money** to the **Temple**. Some gave **lots** of money, but there was a **poor widow** who gave the **little** she had.

  Widows were very vulnerable in Jesus's society. They had no-one to protect them or provide for them — there was no help from the government.

- The **rich** donated only **spare money**, so Jesus said the **widow's gift** was **more valuable**: *"They all gave out of their wealth; but she, out of her poverty, put in everything — all she had to live on"* (Mark 12:44 NIV).

> The widow had **faith** that God would **provide** for her. This story helped **early Christians** believe that God would **provide** for them too if they had complete **faith** in him. It also shows that the **poor** are **important** to God — Christians should **help** them.

A woman anoints Jesus with expensive perfume (14:1-9)

- Jesus was with **Simon the Leper** when a woman tipped a jar of **expensive perfume** over Jesus's **head**.

  As well as Jesus's appreciation of this woman's actions, the story also shows Jesus's respect for lepers.

- People were **angry** with her — it was **valuable** perfume that could have been used to **help** the **poor**. But Jesus **defended** her. He said she had **prepared** his body for **burial** — this was just before his death.
- He said, *"The poor you will always have with you, and you can help them any time you want. But you will not always have me"* (Mark 14:7 NIV).

Don't disregard these stories — they're important...

Explain two ways in which St Mark's accounts of Jesus and the outcasts are important for Christians today. You should include references from Mark's Gospel. [5]

Theme H — St Mark's Gospel as a Source of Religious, Moral and Spiritual Truths

Faith and Discipleship

The disciples were Jesus's **devoted followers** during his lifetime. The **Twelve** were the most important.

Jesus first called four disciples to follow him (1:16-20)

- Simon (later called **Peter**) and **Andrew** were brothers who were **fishermen** on the Sea of Galilee. Jesus said to them:

> **"Come, follow me... and I will send you out to fish for people"** *Mark 1:17 NIV*

Jesus meant that they would tell people God's message.

They immediately **left** their work behind and **went** with him.

- Jesus also called **James** and **John**, two more fishermen, to go with him. They *"left their father Zebedee in the boat"* (Mark 1:20 NIV) — their faith was so **strong** that they left both **work** and **family** behind.

Discipleship means learning and following

- The number of disciples grew — there were **twelve** who were especially **important** to Jesus.

 Twelve was symbolic of the twelve tribes of Israel in the Old Testament. By choosing twelve disciples, Jesus suggested they were the new chosen people of God.

- 'Disciple' meant the **pupil** of a teacher, or the **apprentice** of a master craftsman, so the disciples **learned** from **Jesus**. It also meant **following** his **life** and his **example**.

> The first disciples show **modern Christians** the level of faith **expected** of them. They **sacrificed** their livelihoods and followed Jesus **without** asking any **questions**.
> - People **nowadays** might be a disciple by following a **vocation** to work for **God**, for example being a **priest**.
> - Others might carry out what Jesus **taught** people, for example by being **kind** and **helping** those in need.

Jesus told the Twelve to preach and heal (6:7-13)

- Jesus told his disciples to go out in **pairs** to **preach**, **heal** the sick and drive out **demons**.

- They took **no food**, **money** or **luggage** — they were to rely on the **hospitality** of others. If they **weren't** made **welcome** somewhere, Jesus said to **leave** and *"shake the dust off your feet as a testimony against them"* (Mark 6:11 NIV). These people had had their chance to hear the **message** — the disciples should spend **no more time** there.

- Jesus spent most of his **ministry** like this, so the disciples were **sharing** his **mission**, showing their **faith** that God would **provide** for them.

MISSION
- Early Christians were encouraged by this during their missionary journeys throughout the Roman Empire.
- Mission in the 21st century is similar — it usually involves practical help as well as preaching. **Christian Aid** and **CAFOD** are Christian organisations which give practical help where needed in foreign countries.

Faith and Discipleship

Discipleship has costs as well as rewards (8:34-38 and 10:28-31)

- Jesus said his **disciples** must *"take up their cross and follow me"* (Mark 8:34 NIV).

  He was saying they might suffer and die, as he was going to.

- But anyone who showed **faith** and **gave** things **up** for Jesus would be **rewarded** both on **Earth** and in **heaven**:

> *"...no one who has left home... for me and the gospel will fail to receive a hundred times as much in this present age... and in the age to come eternal life. But many who are first will be last, and the last first"* Mark 10:29-31 NIV

- Although they'd given up family, they'd have a huge new family of Jesus's followers.
- They may have been treated badly on Earth, but in heaven it'd be them, rather than their persecutors, who were respected.

Early Christians would have been **comforted** by this.

- Those who opted for an easy life instead would **lose** their **future life** in the **kingdom of God**. Anyone who **disowned** him would **later** be disowned by **Jesus** on the **Day of Judgement**.

> Modern Christians are less likely to face the same **suffering** as Jesus's early followers, but they must still be prepared to **give up** their own **wishes** and be ready for **hardship** rather than an **easy life** when they "take up their cross".

Jesus heals a woman who is bleeding heavily (5:24-34)

- A woman who had been suffering from a haemorrhage for **12 years** approached Jesus in a crowd and **secretly** touched his **cloak**. She believed it would **heal** her and it did.

  haemorrhage
  excessive bleeding

- Jesus felt **power** leave him. He **asked** who had touched him and the woman **owned up**.

- The **bleeding** meant the woman would have been seen as **unclean**, and by **touching** Jesus she would have made him **unclean** too, but that **didn't** concern him. Jesus said to her: *"Daughter, your faith has healed you. Go in peace and be freed from your suffering"* (Mark 5:34 NIV).

FAITH
- The woman in the story was **healed** because she had **faith**. Jesus often said this when he healed people.
- Faith in Mark's Gospel means **trusting God** — and **acting on** that trust.
- The woman acted by **seeking out** Jesus and **touching** him. This story shows the **importance** of **faith** for Christians.

The disciples spread Jesus's teachings...

...but have they taught you anything? Give this exam-style question a go and see.
Give two examples of how people in the 21st century might carry out their discipleship. [2]

Theme H — St Mark's Gospel as a Source of Religious, Moral and Spiritual Truths

Faith and Discipleship

Peter denies he is one of Jesus's disciples (14:27-31, 66-72)

- Just before his arrest, Jesus predicted that **all** of the disciples would **desert** him.
  Peter insisted he **wouldn't**, even if everyone else did. But Jesus said:

> **"today... before the cock crows twice you yourself will disown me three times"** *Mark 14:30 NIV*

Each disciple **swore** he would rather **die** than **desert** Jesus.

- After Jesus was **arrested**, Peter was challenged **three times** in the courtyard outside where Jesus was being held. Each time, he **denied** being one of Jesus's **disciples**.

> **"I don't know this man you're talking about."** *Mark 14:71 NIV*

- Then he heard the cock **crow twice**, and **recalled** what Jesus had said. He was very **upset**.

> **"he broke down and wept"** *Mark 14:72 NIV*

Mark considered Peter to be the **unofficial leader** of the **disciples** — he was the **first** to declare Jesus as the **Messiah**. But out of fear, even Peter **deserted** Jesus in his hour of **need**. This is a **warning** for Christians of the need for **God's help** to remain **faithful**. It **reassures** them that even the **best** Christians **fail** sometimes.

Jesus sent his disciples out and ascended to heaven (16:14-20)

- Jesus **appeared** to the disciples after his **resurrection**. There were only **eleven** of them — **Judas** (who had betrayed him) had **gone**.

- Jesus told them off for **not believing** the people who had seen him **alive**.

> **"he rebuked them for their lack of faith"** *Mark 16:14 NIV*

- He **commissioned** them to tell everyone about the **gospel** and to **baptise** converts.

> **"Whoever believes and is baptised will be saved, but whoever does not believe will be condemned."** *Mark 16:16 NIV*

- He predicted many **miraculous signs** would accompany their preaching. Then Jesus **ascended** to **heaven** to be with God.

- The disciples did as Jesus had **commanded** and **miraculous things** did happen — e.g. **St Paul** was **bitten** by a poisonous snake, but **survived**.
- This encourages modern Christians to **continue** the disciples' **work** — God will **protect** them while they do so. Some **Pentecostal** Churches handle **poisonous snakes** in worship as a **test of faith**.

Mark's Gospel suggests only Christians will be saved

- **Jesus's commission** to his disciples could be understood to mean that **only Christians** will be **saved**. However, verses 9-20 **weren't** included in some **original versions** of the Gospel.

- Many modern Christians **reject** this idea. They think that **other religions** can also be **paths to God**. They also respect **good people** who have **no religion**.

- **Excluding** some people could encourage **prejudice** and **discrimination**. The **rest** of Mark's Gospel is **against** both of these, and there are **laws** in the UK making discrimination **illegal** (see p.104).

REVISION TASK

And that's the end of Mark's Gospel...

One of the best ways to check your understanding of something is to explain it to someone else. Try telling your friends or family about Jesus's disciples and see how much you can remember.

Theme H — St Mark's Gospel as a Source of Religious, Moral and Spiritual Truths

Revision Summary

That's the final section done and dusted, so let's see what you've **learnt**. The **questions** below are like the ones you'll have to answer in the **exam**, so this is a good chance to **practise**. If there's anything you **can't** answer, **go back** through the section and have **another go** when you've re-read it. For some questions — you'll be told which ones — there are **extra marks** for **spelling**, **punctuation** and **grammar**, so check your writing carefully.

Nice and easy to start off with — some 1 mark multiple choice questions.

1) Who did Jesus see giving all they had to the Temple?
   a) A disciple   b) A Gentile   c) A widow   d) A rich man

2) What was the occupation of Jesus's first four disciples?
   a) Tax collector   b) Soldier   c) Fisherman   d) Farmer

3) Who touched Jesus's cloak so that they would be healed?
   a) A leper   b) An epileptic boy   c) A young child   d) A bleeding woman

4) What was the name of the disciple who disowned Jesus when he was arrested?
   a) Levi   b) Peter   c) Judas   d) John

Doubling up to two marks now. All you need to do is make two short points.

5) Give two examples of parables which Jesus told about the kingdom of God.

6) Give two types of people considered outcasts in Jesus's society.

7) Give two examples of how Jesus's attitude towards outcasts is reflected in modern society.

8) Give two examples of what was expected of Jesus's disciples.

Rising to 4 marks per question. You have to develop your points to get them all.

9) Explain two contrasting beliefs about Jesus's instruction to
   "sell everything you have and give to the poor" (Mark 10:21 NIV).

10) Explain two contrasting 1st century beliefs about people with illnesses.

11) Explain two contrasting beliefs held by modern Christians about what discipleship means.

12) Explain two contrasting interpretations of Jesus's commission to his disciples.

And some more questions — this time for 5 marks. You'll need to give references from St Mark's Gospel.

13) Explain two ways in which St Mark's account of the parable of the sower is important for Christians today.

14) Explain two ways in which St Mark's account of Jesus's treatment of children is important for Christians today.

15) Explain two ways in which St Mark's account of the greatest commandments is important for Christians today.

16) Explain two ways in which St Mark's account of Peter's denial is important for Christians today.

Drum roll please... it's time for the 12 mark question (along with an extra 3 marks for SPaG). The exam question will have a list of points you need to make in your answer, so use it to plan things out first. Write down arguments for and against the statement so you don't forget any while writing your answer.

17) 'The kingdom of God has already come.'
    Evaluate this statement.
    Your answer should include the following:
    - references to Mark's Gospel
    - arguments that support the statement
    - arguments that disagree with the statement
    - a conclusion

'References to Mark's Gospel' means either quotations, paraphrasing or chapter and verse references.

Theme H — St Mark's Gospel as a Source of Religious, Moral and Spiritual Truths

Do Well in Your Exam

You've learnt all the **facts** — now it's time to get those **grades**.

You'll sit two exams which are worth 50% each

This information is for the full course. For the short course you'll just sit one exam.

You'll sit **two** exam papers: **Paper 1** is about religious **beliefs**, **teachings** and **practices**, and **Paper 2** is about the **thematic studies**.

- Both papers are **1 hour and 45 minutes** long, and they're each worth **50%** of your **overall mark**.

Paper 1

- For Paper 1, you'll be given **two booklets**, one for each of the two religions you've studied. If you've done the textual studies on **St Mark's Gospel**, you'll answer questions on **Christianity** or **Catholic Christianity**, plus **one other religion**.
- There'll be **2** questions in **each** booklet, with each **broken down** into **5** parts.
- Try to spend around **50 minutes** on each religion.

Paper 2

- In Paper 2, you need to answer the questions for the **four themes** you've studied. If you've done the textual studies on **St Mark's Gospel** (Themes G and H), you'll choose questions on the **two** religious, philosophical and ethical themes you've covered (Themes A-F), then the **two** themes on Mark's Gospel.
- There'll be **1** question **per** theme, which will be **divided** into **5** parts.
- Aim to work on **each** theme for roughly **25 minutes**.

The basics — read the questions

- **Read** the questions **carefully**. Remember to answer **all the parts** of the questions.
- Be aware of how much **time** you're using. Leave plenty of time for the long-answer questions. The more **marks** a question's worth, the **longer** you should be spending on it — for these exams, allow around **1 minute per mark**. Try to leave yourself 5 minutes at the end to **check your work**.
- Some questions will have extra marks available for **Spelling, Punctuation and Grammar** (SPaG) — there are 6 SPaG marks available in **Paper 1** and 3 SPaG marks in **Paper 2**. The exam paper will tell you which questions offer SPaG marks — so make your writing for these the best it can be (see p.113 for more).
- Don't use any fancy colours — write **only** in **black** ink.

1 mark questions are always multiple choice

The 1 mark questions are pretty **straightforward** — read **all** the options before you make your choice. If you're **not sure**, **guess** — you won't lose any marks.

> Which of the following is the name of the pillar of Islam that means giving money to charity?
>
> a) Hajj   b) Salah   c) Shahadah   d) Zakah

The correct answer is d) **Zakah**.

'Twas the night before the exam...

...and some people were up late, studying RS. Make sure you get a good night's rest before your exam — you won't be able to do your best if you're half asleep.

Do Well in Your Exam

There are some subtle differences between the question types, so make sure you're clear what's what.

2 mark questions just need two brief points

- The two mark questions will ask for **two** points on a particular topic. You could be asked for two **beliefs**, **examples**, **reasons**, **ways** — e.g. examples of how religious believers might act, reasons why something is important or influences believers, or ways that believers celebrate something.
- Keep your answers **short** and **to the point** — you **don't** need to write in **full sentences**.

> Give two religious beliefs about divorce.

Many religious people think that divorce should be the last resort. Roman Catholics think that divorce is impossible. ⟵ Don't be tempted to **write lots**.

For the **Paper 2** questions, your points can be **general** or about a **specific religion**.

4 mark questions might ask how beliefs influence people

- The **four mark** question in the 'Beliefs' section of **Paper 1** will ask you to **explain** how a particular belief **influences** religious people.
- Make **two points**, but you'll have to **develop** them in order to get **full marks**.

> Explain two ways in which believing in the Trinity influences modern Christians.

The **first sentence here** **introduces** the influence, and the **second** sentence **builds** on that point. ⟶ Christians believe that Jesus set the example for how Christians should act. By reading the Gospels, they can learn more about his life and how they should behave.
Christians believe the Holy Spirit guides them personally and the Church as a whole. They think the Spirit can help them to follow God's teachings and to live in the way God intended.

4 mark questions might ask for similar or contrasting views

- The **four mark** questions in the 'Practices' section of **Paper 1** and all of **Paper 2** will ask you to explain either two **similar** or two **contrasting** views about a topic.
- Be sure to read the **whole question**. For some 'contrasting' questions on Themes A-F, you'll be asked to write about views from **one or more religious traditions** — you can **pick** the religions.
- For others you must answer about the **main religious tradition** in the UK (**Christianity**) and **another** religious tradition. You **don't** have to write about **different religions** here — you could write about two contrasting views from **within Christianity**, e.g. from **different denominations**.

> Explain two contrasting beliefs in Britain today about forgiveness.
> You must refer to the main religious tradition in the UK and at least one other religious viewpoint.

Forgiveness is important to many Christians. They believe that God is always prepared to forgive sins, and Christians should accept his forgiveness and follow his example.
In Islam, some sins are seen as being so terrible that they can't be forgiven. For example, if someone commits shirk, this is considered unforgivable.

Don't let exam nerves get the better of you...

A large chunk of how well you do in the exam comes down to, well... how good you are at exams. Make sure you spend enough time practising doing exam-style questions under timed conditions. It'll pay off in the end.

Do Well in Your Exam

For 5 mark questions you must be able to refer to sacred texts

- The **five mark** questions ask you to **explain** two things, such as beliefs, teachings, ways that believers act, or reasons why something is important.
- You need to give two points and **develop** them, but for full marks you must **refer** to a **sacred text** or religious **teaching**. This could be by including a **quotation**, or by **paraphrasing** (explaining what's said in your own words). You'll need to say which text or teaching the information **comes from**. For the **Bible**, you need to say which **book** you're referring to, e.g. Genesis.

> Explain two Muslim teachings on jihad.
> Your answer should refer to religious texts.

> There's only **one mark** available for referring to religious texts, so **one quote or reference** will do.

> You could also write something like 'The Qur'an gives Muslims permission to defend themselves if they're being fought'.

> Greater jihad is the struggle to live life according to Allah's teachings. It's a personal struggle, and individuals must work to be the best Muslims they can be. Lesser jihad can involve defending Islam. This could be in a peaceful way, or by fighting a threat to Islam in self-defence. The Qur'an says: "Permission [to fight] has been given to those who are being fought".

For 12 mark questions you need both sides of the argument

For the **12 mark** question, you'll need to write a **longer answer**. You'll be given a **statement** and a **list** of bullet points — these tell you what to put in your answer.

- You need to give arguments **for** and **against** the statement, so read it carefully, then make a rough list of all the **views** on each side that you can think of.
- **Plan** out your answer **before** you start writing — it needs to be **clear** and **organised** for the examiner.
- Here's an example of a **question** and **answer** from **Paper 2**:

> 'Animal experimentation should be allowed if it benefits humanity.'
> Evaluate this statement. Your answer should include the following:
> - religious arguments that support the statement
> - religious arguments that disagree with the statement
> - a conclusion
> You can also include non-religious points of view in your answer.

> The points in **Paper 1** are a bit **different**. They'll ask you to include **teachings** from the **religion** you've studied, arguments **for** and **against**, and a **conclusion**.

> Many religious believers share this point of view. They believe that animal testing is acceptable if it is for valid reasons, such as producing life-saving medicines. Testing cosmetics on animals wouldn't be considered acceptable. They also think that the animals must be treated humanely, and no unnecessary pain caused. Many religious people see themselves as stewards of the Earth, and believe they must look after animals.

> This answer starts by giving some **general views** that **agree** with the statement.

> Some religious teachings allow animal experimentation. The Catechism of the Catholic Church says that animal testing is allowed if it brings about scientific or medical advances, but the animals shouldn't be allowed to suffer.

> The second paragraph gets more specific and references **religious ideas** and **texts**.

> Some people might look at animal testing from a utilitarian point of view. If testing on animals would produce the best balance of good and bad outcomes, they would argue it is allowed.

> The third paragraph explains how **ethics** influence views.

> However, not all religious believers would support this view. Some people, such as the Society of Friends (Quakers), are against causing any kind of suffering to animals. They would think it's wrong to inflict pain on animals just to further our knowledge of science and medicine.

> This paragraph discusses arguments **against** the statement.

> You would need to include **more** here — this part of the answer **isn't finished**.

> . . . .

> I think that, although allowing animals to suffer is wrong, if the experiments could benefit humanity then they should be allowed. As for what is considered beneficial, any medical or scientific advances that could save human lives would be acceptable, but testing non-essential products such as cosmetics would not be a good enough reason to carry out animal testing. The Bible and the Qur'an say that animals should be looked after well, so any inessential suffering in the experiment would be unacceptable.

> Finish with a **conclusion** — say what **you** think, and **back it up** with ideas you've discussed. These sentences should give you an idea — but you'd need to say a bit **more** in the real thing.

Spelling, Punctuation and Grammar

You get marks in your exams for having good **SPaG** (Spelling, Punctuation and Grammar). It might not be particularly thrilling but if you can get it right, it's **easy marks**. This page is about checking your work...

Some 12 mark questions have 3 extra marks for SPaG

- In **Paper 1**, **3 marks** are available for spelling, punctuation and grammar in the **12 mark question** on 'Beliefs', for **each** of your two religions — so that's **6 SPaG** marks available in total for Paper 1. For **Paper 2**, up to **3 SPaG marks** are available for **each** 12 mark question — but it's only the **highest** SPaG mark you get across your four 12 mark questions that's counted. So that's **3 SPaG marks** available for Paper 2, meaning you could get **up to 9 marks** across the two exams just for SPaG.

- The examiner will look at your spelling, punctuation and grammar **generally**, but they'll also look at how many **technical terms** you use and how **accurately** you use them.

- Leave **5 minutes** at the end of the exam to **check your work**. That **isn't** long, so there **won't** be time to check **everything** thoroughly. Look for the **most obvious** mistakes.

- **Start** by checking the **12 mark** questions since they're the **only ones** that award SPaG marks. **Only** check the rest of your answers if you've got **time**.

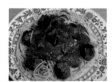

My favourite kind of SPaG...

Check for common spelling mistakes

When you're writing under pressure, it's easy to let spelling mistakes creep in, but there are a few things you can watch out for:

Check for missing words as well as misspelt words.

- Look out for words which **sound the same** but **mean different things** and are **spelt differently**. Make sure you've used the correct one. For example, 'their', 'there' and 'they're':

> The Bible says that wives should do what their husbands say.

> There are many conditions that must be met for a war to be 'just'.

> Some people might commit crime because they're living in poverty.

- **Don't** use text speak, and always write words out **in full**. For example, use **'and'** instead of '**&**' or '**+**'. **Don't** use 'etc.' when you could give **more examples** or a **better explanation**.

- Make sure you've used the appropriate **technical terms** (like 'euthanasia', 'sacrament' or 'Shari'ah'). If they're **spelt correctly**, it'll really **impress** the **examiner**.

Make sure your grammar and punctuation are correct

- Check you've used **capital letters**, **full stops** and **question marks** correctly.

- Make sure your writing **isn't too chatty** and doesn't use **slang words**. It should be **formal**.

- Watch out for sentences where your writing switches between **different tenses**. You should usually use **one tense** throughout your answer (don't worry if you've used a quote that's in a different tense though).

- Check that you've started a **new paragraph** every time you make a new point. It's important that your answer **isn't** just **one long block** of text.

- Watch out for tricksy little **grammar mistakes**:
  - Remember — '**it's**' (with an apostrophe) is short for '**it is**' or '**it has**'. '**Its**' (without an apostrophe) means '**belonging to it**'.
  - It's always '**should have**', not 'should of' (the same goes for 'could have' and 'would have' too).

  If you know that you **often** confuse two words, like 'it's' and 'its', **watch out** for them when you're checking your work in the exam.

Thou shalt use correct punctuation...

There's a lot of stuff to check, which is why it's really important to get to grips with it all and practise before the exam. That way you'll start to do it automatically, and make fewer errors in the first place.

Glossary and Index

The orange definitions are relevant to Christianity and Catholic Christianity.
The green ones are terms in Islam. The blue ones are general terms.

abortion	Removing a foetus from the womb before it is able to survive, ending the pregnancy. **51-53**	
adultery	A married person having sex with someone who isn't their husband or wife. **39, 76**	
Advent	The period of time that begins four Sundays before Christmas. 18	
Al-Adab al-Mufrad	A collection of hadith. 88	
al-Akhirah	The concept of life after death. This is a key Islamic belief. 30	
al-Qadr	Predestination — the idea that Allah has already decided everything that will happen. 30	
the ascension	When Jesus rose up to heaven to be with God again. 10, 108	
atheism	A complete denial of the existence of a god. **56, 61, 62 65**	
atonement	Making amends for wrongdoing — often refers to people repairing their relationship with God. **10, 11**	
barzakh	Where souls wait for Yawm ad-Din (the Day of Judgement). 30, 54	
benevolent	Being kind and loving. **2, 5, 7, 26, 58, 62**	
capital punishment	The death penalty as punishment for a crime. **78**	
catechism	A set of statements explaining the teachings of the Catholic Church. 8, 15, 37, 38, 41, 42, 45, 82, 85	
celibacy	Not taking part in any sexual activities. **37**	
cohabitation	Living together in a sexual relationship without being married. **37, 39, 40**	
confession	Admitting sins to God/Allah. **12, 15, 16**	
confirmation	The act of 'confirming' your faith, often at an age when you can decide for yourself. 14, 15, 42	
conscience	An inner feeling of what's right and what's wrong. **38, 41, 59, 64**	
contraception	Also known as birth control, it stops a woman from conceiving. **38**	
corporal punishment	Punishing a criminal through physical pain. **77**	
covenant	A formal agreement between two or more people. **59, 97**	
creed	Statement of religious beliefs. 3, 12, 16	
disciples	Followers of Jesus (either in the Bible, or all Christians) 9, 10, 92-97, 101-104, 106-108	
discrimination	Treating different people, or groups of people, differently (usually unfairly). **44, 45, 80, 84, 104, 105**	
dominion	The belief that people have power over God's creation and can use it as they like. 5, 49, 50	
the Eucharist	When Christians remember the Last Supper with bread and wine. 10, 12-15, 92, 97	
euthanasia	Ending someone's life to relieve their suffering, especially from an incurable, painful illness. **51-53**	
evangelism	Spreading the Christian message in order to convert people. 21	
fasting	Not eating and/or drinking for a set time. **19, 33, 35**	
free will	The ability to choose how to behave. Both religions believe humans have free will. **6, 7, 30, 62, 72**	
Gethsemane	The garden where Jesus prayed before his arrest. 10, 97	
Golgotha	The 'place of the skull' where Jesus was crucified. 10, 98	
grace	God showing favour to those who haven't earned it. 8, 11, 14, 15	
hadith	Islamic scripture containing a collection of things the Prophet Muhammad said and did. 29	
hajj	The pilgrimage to Makkah. 31, 34, 80	

Glossary

Glossary and Index

Glossary and Index

Glossary